IMPORTANT NOTICE

This guide provides comprehensive and reliable information, designed to help travelers explore the destination with confidence. Nevertheless, it does not substitute for official sources or professional advice issued by relevant authorities. Travelers are encouraged to stay updated on local regulations, safety protocols, and guidelines to ensure a safe, smooth, and enjoyable journey.

CW01499391

TABLE OF CONTENTS

Chapter 1: Welcome to the French Alps

1.1 Why the French Alps Remain a Timeless Destination

Few destinations in Europe inspire the same sense of wonder as the French Alps. These mountains, stretching across southeastern France and bordering Switzerland and Italy, have captivated travelers for centuries. In 2025–2026, they remain a cornerstone of European travel, a place where snow-dusted peaks meet turquoise lakes, and ancient villages coexist with cosmopolitan resort towns. The Alps are not only about skiing, although the region is globally recognized for its legendary slopes. They also offer a four-season playground, attracting hikers, food lovers, culture seekers, and wellness travelers.

The enduring appeal of the French Alps lies in their diversity. Travelers who crave adrenaline find world-class ski runs, off-piste adventures, and extreme sports like paragliding or canyoning. Families discover villages where children can safely play in mountain meadows or learn to ski on gentle slopes. Couples are drawn to Annecy's canals or Chamonix's panoramic views, while budget travelers find affordable mountain refuges and hostel networks. Luxury visitors indulge in chalets with private chefs, spas overlooking glaciers, and Michelin-starred dining.

Another reason the French Alps remain timeless is their accessibility. High-speed trains link Paris and Lyon directly to alpine towns, airports connect visitors to Europe and beyond, and well-planned bus networks make remote valleys reachable without a car. Unlike some mountain regions where infrastructure feels outdated, the French Alps balance modern convenience with authenticity.

The Alps also hold a cultural richness that rivals their natural beauty. The food scene blends rustic tradition with modern creativity, while festivals celebrate everything from music to local harvests. The region is proud of its heritage, reflected in wooden chalets, village festivals, and a deep respect for alpine life. This combination of scenery, culture, accessibility, and year-round experiences makes the French Alps as relevant for the traveler of 2025 as they were for the mountaineers of a century ago.

1.2 What's New in 2025–2026: Emerging Trends & Openings

The French Alps are never static. Each year brings innovations, shifts in traveler expectations, and new opportunities. Entering 2025–2026, several developments stand out for visitors:

Sustainable Travel at the Forefront
Many resorts are moving toward carbon-neutral goals. Les Arcs and Avoriaz are among those leading with solar-powered lifts, green-certified accommodations, and reduced car zones. In Chamonix, new eco-shuttle systems have been introduced to cut down traffic within the valley, making it easier to travel without renting a car.

Wellness and Slow Travel
Travelers in 2025 are increasingly looking for balance. Spas that combine alpine traditions with modern therapies are thriving. Thermal towns such as Aix-les-Bains and Saint-Gervais-les-Bains are drawing visitors for week-long wellness retreats, often combined with yoga or hiking programs. This shift shows that the Alps are not only for adrenaline seekers but also for those who want to recharge.

Digital Nomadism in the Mountains

The rise of remote work has changed alpine tourism. Co-working chalets in Annecy, Grenoble, and Morzine now offer high-speed internet with mountain views, attracting nomads who stay for weeks or even months. Towns have adapted by offering seasonal rental packages, and cafés increasingly provide work-friendly environments.

Culinary Evolution

Alpine cuisine is experiencing a modern renaissance. While fondue and raclette remain staples, chefs are experimenting with plant-based menus and farm-to-table dining. Several new Michelin-starred restaurants opened in 2024–2025, blending traditional mountain flavors with global influences. Food lovers visiting in 2025–2026 will notice more diversity and innovation than ever before.

Improved Transport Links

Travel within the Alps has become more seamless. A new TGV route between Lyon and Annecy reduces travel time, while bus networks connecting smaller towns are expanding. Electric car rentals and e-bike stations are now common, reflecting a broader push toward sustainable mobility.

Cultural Highlights

Major festivals are adapting to growing international audiences. The Annecy International Animation Festival in 2025 will feature an expanded program with open-air screenings along the lake, while Chamonix is set to host new cultural events blending art, science, and mountaineering history.

For travelers, these changes mean more choice, easier access, and experiences that align with the values of sustainability and well-being. Visiting in 2025–2026 offers the chance to enjoy both the timeless beauty of the Alps and the modern comforts shaping its future.

1.3 Geography & Regions at a Glance

The French Alps cover a vast area, stretching across several departments. Understanding the regions helps travelers plan effectively, since each area has its own personality and strengths.

Haute-Savoie
Home to Mont Blanc and the town of Chamonix, Haute-Savoie is perhaps the most iconic alpine region. Annecy, often called the "Venice of the Alps," also lies here, with its canals and turquoise lake. Haute-Savoie combines adventure, culture, and romance, making it a favorite for first-time visitors.

Savoie
 South of Haute-Savoie, this region is famous for its ski resorts. Les Trois Vallées, Val d'Isère, and Méribel are here, offering some of the largest ski domains in the world. Beyond skiing, Savoie is rich in food culture, especially cheeses like Beaufort and Tomme.

Isère

Anchored by Grenoble, Isère is both cultural and adventurous. The city is known for museums, research centers, and access to several ski areas. It is also a gateway for hiking, cycling, and climbing. Travelers seeking a blend of urban life and mountain exploration often base themselves here.

Hautes-Alpes

Quieter and less developed than the northern Alps, this region offers sun-drenched valleys and authentic alpine life. Queyras Regional Park is ideal for hiking, while Serre Chevalier is a well-regarded ski area. The Hautes-Alpes suit those who want fewer crowds.

Ain and Drôme

Though technically on the edges of the Alps, these regions provide a transition between alpine landscapes and the Rhône Valley. Vineyards, gentle mountains, and charming towns make them excellent for travelers combining mountain adventure with wine tourism.

Together, these regions provide more than one trip could cover. For many visitors, the choice depends on priorities: skiing, culture, relaxation, or exploration.

1.4 Who the French Alps Are For: Matching Trips to Traveler Types

The French Alps are versatile, but how they are experienced depends on the traveler. Matching your travel style to the right area or activity makes all the difference.

Solo Travelers
The Alps are safe, well-connected, and social. Hostels in Annecy or Chamonix create natural meeting points, while guided hikes and ski lessons provide opportunities to connect with others. Solo travelers benefit from the structured activities and the friendliness of mountain communities.

Couples
Romantic moments are abundant. Imagine strolling by Lake Annecy at sunset, sharing a private chalet in Megève, or soaking in thermal baths together. Couples will also enjoy fine dining options, wine tours, and secluded mountain lodges.

Families with Children
The Alps are family-friendly, with resorts offering ski schools, childcare, and gentle slopes. Summer brings safe hiking trails and lakeside beaches. Towns like Les Gets have developed reputations as

ideal family bases with activities designed for children.

Budget Travelers and Backpackers

While the Alps can be expensive, they also offer hostels, affordable mountain huts, and camping options. Regional transport passes help keep costs down, and self-catering is easy thanks to markets and supermarkets. Backpackers often choose Grenoble or Annecy as affordable bases.

Luxury Seekers

The French Alps are one of Europe's premier luxury destinations. Exclusive ski resorts like Courchevel offer chalets with private chefs and spa facilities. Michelin-starred restaurants, helicopter tours, and private mountain guides cater to high-end tastes.

Adventure Travelers

Thrill-seekers will never be bored. Winter offers skiing, snowboarding, and ice climbing. Summer introduces mountaineering, via ferrata, rafting, and paragliding. With well-marked trails and professional guides, adventure travelers find opportunities at every turn.

Digital Nomads

With co-working hubs and reliable internet, the Alps are now on the remote-work map. Cities like Annecy and Grenoble blend lifestyle and infrastructure, while smaller towns are experimenting with work-friendly accommodations. For nomads seeking both productivity and adventure, the Alps are an increasingly appealing option.

1.5 How to Use This Guide

This book is designed to be more than a list of recommendations. It is structured as a companion that helps you navigate the French Alps like a local insider, ensuring that every step of your journey is informed and enjoyable.

Each chapter focuses on a core aspect of travel. You will find practical information such as transport details, budgeting strategies, and safety tips. Alongside these, immersive sections explore food, culture, traditions, and local experiences. Seasonal advice is included so you know when to plan for skiing, hiking, or festivals.

Throughout the guide, you will notice sections highlighting hidden gems. These are places less likely to appear in mainstream itineraries but which capture the authentic spirit of the Alps. There are also suggestions for day trips and cross-border excursions, allowing you to connect your Alpine journey with destinations in Italy, Switzerland, or southern France.

Practical travelers will find checklists, cost breakdowns, and insider tips designed to save time and money. Those seeking cultural depth will discover explanations of festivals, customs, and everyday alpine etiquette. Adventure travelers will find detailed descriptions of activities, while digital nomads will benefit from insights into connectivity and long-term stays.

Most importantly, the guide is written for 2025–2026. Trends, new openings, and future developments are included so your trip feels current rather than dated. Whether you are planning months in advance or making last-minute choices, the book equips you with knowledge to travel confidently.

Use this guide as a tool to design your own journey. Read it sequentially if you want a full picture of the Alps, or dip into specific chapters based on your interests. Either way, it is intended to give you both clarity and inspiration, ensuring your time in the French Alps is memorable and tailored to you.

Chapter 2: When to Visit: Seasons, Weather & Events

The French Alps are a destination that truly transforms with the seasons. From snow-dusted ski resorts to flower-filled meadows, from lakeside picnics to wine harvest celebrations, every time of year offers a distinct way to experience the mountains. Unlike many destinations that shine brightest in just one season, the Alps are year-round and endlessly versatile. The key is to understand how each season shapes the landscape, the culture, and the kinds of activities available. This chapter will help you decide when to visit based on your interests, travel style, and budget.

2.1 Winter Wonderland: Ski Season & Christmas Magic

Winter is when the French Alps live up to their most iconic reputation: Europe's ultimate ski playground. From December through March, snow blankets the slopes, villages twinkle with festive lights, and the crisp mountain air brings travelers from across the globe.

The Ski Season
 The peak ski season usually runs from mid-December to late March, though higher-altitude resorts such as Val Thorens or Tignes often extend into April thanks to their glacier skiing. Resorts like Chamonix, Les Trois Vallées, and La Plagne welcome skiers of all levels, with well-groomed pistes, off-piste challenges, and family-friendly beginner zones.

Atmosphere & Scenery
Alpine villages come alive in winter with a fairy-tale feel. Wooden chalets are adorned with snow, fireplaces crackle in cozy restaurants, and après-ski culture is in full swing. Whether you are carving down black diamond runs or sipping mulled wine in a mountain bar, winter in the Alps offers an unmatched combination of sport and atmosphere.

Christmas & New Year

December brings one of the most enchanting times to visit. Christmas markets pop up in towns like Annecy, Grenoble, and Chambéry, selling artisan crafts, local cheeses, and vin chaud. Resorts often host torchlight descents, fireworks, and concerts to celebrate both Christmas and New Year's Eve. Families especially appreciate the festive programming, with Santa appearances, sleigh rides, and kid-friendly shows.

Who It's Best For

- Skiers and snowboarders of all levels.

- Families seeking a festive winter holiday.

- Luxury travelers who want alpine chalets, spas, and gourmet dining.

- Photographers looking to capture snow-covered peaks and alpine lights.

Budget Considerations

Winter is the most expensive season in the Alps, especially during the Christmas and February school holiday periods. Early booking is essential for accommodations. Budget-conscious travelers can save by visiting in January or March, when prices drop but snow conditions remain good.

2.2 Spring Blooms & Shoulder-Season Savings

As the snow melts, the Alps undergo a dramatic transformation. From April through early June, green valleys emerge, wildflowers bloom, and ski resorts transition into hiking and biking hubs.

The Landscape
Spring is the season of renewal. Meadows are covered in alpine flowers, waterfalls roar with snowmelt, and the weather grows increasingly mild. In lower valleys like Annecy and Aix-les-Bains, the lakes become vibrant backdrops for boating, cycling, and picnicking.

Why Visit in Spring
The shoulder season means fewer tourists, lower prices, and a relaxed pace. It is perfect for those who want to avoid crowds yet still enjoy pleasant weather. While some high-altitude passes may still be closed until June, lower hiking trails and lakeside towns are very accessible.

Festivals & Traditions

- **Easter Celebrations**: Alpine towns host processions and festive meals, often featuring lamb and chocolate treats.

- **Annecy's Venetian Carnival (February–March)**: A unique spectacle inspired by Venice's carnival, where masked figures parade through the medieval streets.

- **May Wine Festivals**: Local villages celebrate new vintages with tastings, music, and community feasts.

Traveler Types Who Love Spring

- Couples seeking romantic getaways with quiet charm.

- Families preferring affordable holidays.

- Outdoor lovers ready for early hikes, cycling, and nature walks.

- Budget backpackers avoiding peak-season costs.

Budget Considerations
Spring is one of the most affordable times to visit. Accommodation and flights are significantly cheaper compared to winter and summer, making it a great time for long-term stays or digital nomads looking for a peaceful work base.

2.3 Summer Escapes: Hiking, Lakes & Festivals

From June to September, the French Alps become a paradise for outdoor enthusiasts. Long days, warm weather, and lush landscapes attract hikers, bikers, swimmers, and festival-goers.

Weather & Landscape
 Summer brings clear skies, alpine meadows in full bloom, and pleasant temperatures averaging between 20–30°C in valleys and cooler highs at altitude. This is peak hiking season, with famous trails like the Tour du Mont Blanc drawing adventurers from around the world.

Top Activities

- **Hiking**: Ranging from gentle lakeside walks to multi-day treks.

- **Water Adventures**: Swimming, kayaking, and paddleboarding in lakes such as Annecy, Bourget, and Geneva.

- **Cycling**: Both road cyclists and mountain bikers flock to the Alps, inspired by the Tour de France routes.

- **Paragliding**: Chamonix, Annecy, and Morzine are top spots for soaring over valleys.

Festivals & Events
Summer is also festival season.

- **Musilac Festival (Aix-les-Bains, July)**: A major music event on the lake's edge.

- **Chamonix CosmoJazz Festival (July)**: Outdoor jazz concerts against mountain backdrops.

- **Tour de France (July)**: Cycling fans line the routes to cheer on riders as they tackle alpine passes.

- **Fête du Lac (Annecy, August)**: One of Europe's biggest pyrotechnic shows over Lake Annecy.

Who Thrives in Summer

- Adventure travelers chasing outdoor thrills.

- Families enjoying lake activities and mountain fun.

- Solo travelers drawn to international hiking groups.

- Digital nomads looking for alpine coworking hubs.

Budget Considerations

July and August are high season with peak prices, especially in lakeside towns. Booking early is necessary. Travelers on a budget can save by visiting in late June or early September when crowds thin but the weather remains warm.

2.4 Autumn Colors & Wine Harvests

September to November is a season of calm and beauty in the Alps. Fewer tourists, golden foliage, and culinary delights make autumn a well-kept secret.

The Scenery
 Forests turn brilliant shades of red, orange, and gold, creating some of the most photogenic landscapes of the year. Crisp air and softer light make it perfect for photography and leisurely walks.

Wine & Culinary Festivals
 Autumn is harvest time, and vineyards in regions like Savoie and Isère buzz with activity. Travelers can join grape-picking events, taste local wines such as Jacquère or Mondeuse, and enjoy traditional alpine cuisine prepared with seasonal ingredients like mushrooms and chestnuts.

Best Activities

- Hiking in cooler, quieter conditions.

- Attending village fairs celebrating cheese, apples, or chestnuts.

- Visiting thermal spas for relaxation as the weather cools.

- Exploring historic towns without summer crowds.

Traveler Types Who Love Autumn

- Couples seeking a romantic, tranquil getaway.

- Food and wine enthusiasts.

- Retirees or slow travelers enjoying cultural immersion.

- Photographers chasing autumnal color palettes.

Budget Considerations

Autumn is one of the most cost-effective times to visit. Accommodation discounts are common, and attractions are less crowded. However, some mountain lifts and facilities may close after summer, so plan accordingly.

2.5 Annual Events & Seasonal Highlights

Each year, the French Alps host a variety of events that define the rhythm of the region and attract international visitors. Knowing the calendar helps travelers align their trips with the experiences they want most.

Winter Highlights

- **December**: Christmas markets in Grenoble, Annecy, and Chamonix.

- **January–March**: Major ski competitions, including the Kandahar Alpine Ski World Cup in Chamonix.

- **New Year's Eve**: Torchlit descents and fireworks in ski resorts.

Spring Highlights

- **April–May**: Easter celebrations, spring flower festivals, and local wine events.

- **May**: Cycling events such as the Critérium du Dauphiné, a Tour de France warm-up race.

Summer Highlights

- **July**: Tour de France stages, Musilac Festival, CosmoJazz Festival.

- **August**: Annecy's Fête du Lac fireworks.

- **June–September**: Village fêtes and outdoor concerts across alpine towns.

Autumn Highlights

- **September–October**: Wine harvest festivals in Savoie.

- **October**: Chestnut festivals in Ardèche and nearby regions.

- **November**: Saint Martin's Day celebrations marking the end of harvest.

Insider Tip

Aligning your trip with a festival can add unforgettable experiences, but it also means higher demand for hotels and transport. Book early if you want to attend popular events, or aim for smaller village festivals for a more authentic feel.

Chapter 3: Getting In & Around the Alps

One of the joys of traveling to the French Alps is that the journey itself can be just as memorable as the destination. Whether you soar in on a short flight, glide into a valley by train, or wind your way along alpine roads, the routes into this mountain region are scenic and surprisingly accessible. The Alps may feel remote, but they are well connected to the rest of France and neighboring countries, making them easy to reach year-round. Once you arrive, an equally wide range of transport options opens up, from efficient regional trains to local buses and even electric bike rentals. This chapter takes you through everything you need to know about arriving in the Alps and getting around once you're there.

3.1 Airports & International Connections

The French Alps are served by several airports, both major international hubs and smaller regional gateways. Choosing the right one depends on where you're headed, your budget, and your tolerance for transfers.

Major International Gateways

- **Geneva Airport (Switzerland)**: Although located just across the border, Geneva is the most popular entry point for travelers bound for the northern French Alps, particularly Chamonix, Annecy, and Morzine. It offers extensive global connections and frequent flights from across Europe, North America, and the Middle East. Transfers to alpine towns are straightforward via shuttle buses, trains, or car rentals.

- **Lyon–Saint-Exupéry Airport**: Well positioned for the western and central Alps, Lyon is a strong option if you are heading toward Grenoble, Chambéry, or Les Deux Alpes. It is connected to Paris and other French cities via high-speed rail and has direct flights from major European hubs.

- **Milan Malpensa & Turin Caselle (Italy)**: Both Italian airports are practical for reaching resorts on the southern and eastern side of the Alps, such as Val d'Isère and La Rosière. Many travelers combine an Italian city break with an alpine escape.

Regional Airports

- **Chambéry Airport**: Seasonal flights from the UK and northern Europe land here during winter, offering a direct route for skiers heading to resorts like Méribel, Courchevel, and Val Thorens.

- **Grenoble Alpes–Isère Airport**: Primarily a winter gateway, it sees charter and low-cost flights catering to ski travelers.

- **Annecy Mont-Blanc Airport**: A small airport handling private flights, useful mostly for charter or business travelers.

Tips for Flyers

- Book flights at least three to six months in advance for winter peak season.

- If traveling with skis or snowboards, check baggage policies carefully. Many airlines now charge extra for oversized equipment.

- For eco-conscious travelers, consider flying into Paris, Lyon, or Geneva and continuing by high-speed train instead of connecting flights.

3.2 Scenic Train Journeys: TGV & Regional Rail

France's train network is one of the most efficient and enjoyable ways to reach the Alps. Many travelers prefer rail over flying because it reduces stress, cuts emissions, and often delivers spectacular mountain views.

High-Speed Rail (TGV)
The French TGV system links Paris to several key alpine cities in just a few hours.

- Paris to **Chambéry**: around 3 hours.

- Paris to **Grenoble**: about 3 hours 15 minutes.

- Paris to **Annecy**: roughly 3 hours 45 minutes.

- Paris to **Modane** (for access to Maurienne Valley resorts): around 4 hours.

During ski season, special services such as the **Eurostar Snow Train** connect London directly to Bourg-Saint-Maurice and Moûtiers, reducing the need for airport transfers.

Regional Trains (TER)
Once in the Alps, the TER regional trains link smaller towns and valleys. Examples include:

- Chambéry to Annecy.

- Grenoble to Gap via the scenic Route des Alpes.

- Lyon to Bourg-Saint-Maurice.

These slower trains are excellent for taking in the scenery, particularly routes along lakes or climbing through mountain passes.

Why Choose the Train

- No luggage restrictions compared to flights.

- Direct access to many resort gateways.

- Lower carbon footprint.

- Often less expensive if booked early on SNCF Connect.

Insider Tip
For the most scenic journeys, book a window seat

on daytime services running along Lake Annecy or into the Tarentaise Valley.

3.3 Buses, Transfers & Ride-Sharing Options

If you are traveling without a car, buses and shuttles are often the most affordable way to connect airports, train stations, and alpine resorts.

Airport Shuttles
From Geneva, Lyon, and Grenoble airports, numerous companies run seasonal shuttle services to major ski resorts. These can be booked in advance and are especially convenient for families or groups. Travel time varies from 1.5 hours (Geneva to Chamonix) to around 3 hours (Lyon to Val d'Isère).

Regional Bus Networks
Local bus services cover inter-town journeys, though schedules can be limited outside peak winter and summer seasons. For example:

- **SAT Bus Network** operates routes around Annecy and connections to Geneva.

- **Transisère** serves Grenoble and the surrounding Isère department.

- **Altibus** connects train stations like Chambéry or Bourg-Saint-Maurice to ski resorts.

Ride-Sharing & Carpooling
Carpooling has become increasingly popular in the Alps, especially with the rise of platforms like **BlaBlaCar**, which allows you to share a ride with locals at low cost. It's eco-friendly and often faster than buses.

Budget Tip
Buses are cheaper than trains but may take longer, particularly in winter when snow can cause delays. Always check schedules carefully in advance, as rural services can be infrequent.

3.4 Driving the Alps: Routes, Tolls & Parking

Driving is often the most flexible way to explore the French Alps, especially if you plan to hop between valleys, visit remote villages, or explore outside ski season.

Getting There by Car
From Paris, the drive to Annecy or Grenoble takes around 6–7 hours. From Geneva, many French resorts are reachable within 1–3 hours. Major highways (autoroutes) are well maintained but usually tolled.

Scenic Routes

- **Route des Grandes Alpes**: A legendary summer road trip linking Lake Geneva to the Mediterranean via spectacular alpine passes.

- **Lacets de Montvernier**: A famously winding stretch of road near Saint-Jean-de-Maurienne, popular with cyclists and photographers.

Practicalities

- **Tolls**: Expect tolls on major highways. Payment can be made with credit cards or in cash.

- **Winter Tires & Chains**: As of late 2021, French law requires vehicles traveling in mountainous regions during winter (November to March) to carry snow chains or be fitted with winter tires.

- **Parking**: Larger resorts offer designated car parks, often at the village edge with shuttle buses into the center. Smaller towns may have free or low-cost parking.

Who Should Drive

- Families with young children who need flexibility.

- Travelers with sports gear or multiple bags.

- Those keen on exploring hidden valleys and villages not served by rail or bus.

3.5 Public Transit Within Alpine Towns & Villages

Once you've arrived in your alpine base, getting around locally is usually straightforward. Many towns have invested heavily in sustainable, visitor-friendly transport systems to reduce car use.

Local Buses & Shuttles
Most ski resorts and towns run free or low-cost shuttle buses linking neighborhoods, ski lifts, and nearby villages. For example, Chamonix's "Le Mulet" shuttle provides eco-friendly city transport, while Annecy offers efficient bus routes across town and to the lakeside.

Cycling & E-Bikes
During summer, cycling is one of the best ways to explore alpine towns. E-bike rentals are increasingly common, making even steep climbs accessible to casual riders. Resorts like Morzine and Les Gets have developed extensive mountain bike trails.

Walking-Friendly Centers
Many alpine towns have pedestrianized centers, making walking both practical and pleasant. Annecy's old town, Chamonix's core, and Val

d'Isère's village center are all car-free zones filled with shops, restaurants, and cafés.

Taxis & Ride-Hailing
 Taxis are available but can be expensive, particularly in ski resorts. Ride-hailing services like Uber operate in larger cities such as Grenoble and Lyon but are limited in smaller mountain towns. Local taxi companies are more reliable in remote areas, though pre-booking is advised.

Accessibility
 Efforts have been made in recent years to improve accessibility for travelers with reduced mobility. Many resort shuttle buses are wheelchair-accessible, and lifts often include priority access. Always check with local tourist offices for the latest accessibility updates.

The French Alps may look wild and rugged on the map, but getting in and around is remarkably smooth once you understand the options. Whether you prefer the efficiency of trains, the flexibility of a car, or the eco-friendliness of local shuttles and e-bikes, there is a way of traveling that will suit your style and budget. The key is planning ahead, especially during winter and summer peaks, when demand is highest.

Chapter 4: Budgeting Your French Alps Trip

Planning a trip to the French Alps involves more than picking a resort or a season. The region offers every type of travel experience, from shoestring backpacking through valleys to ultra-luxury chalet stays in world-famous ski towns. Understanding how much to expect for accommodation, food, transport, and activities will help you avoid surprises and make the most of your money. This chapter breaks down typical costs, highlights strategies for different traveler budgets, and shares insider tips for saving where it matters most.

4.1 Cost Breakdown: Accommodation, Food, Transport & Activities

Costs in the Alps vary dramatically by season, destination, and travel style. Below is a 2025–2026 perspective on what you can expect to pay.

Accommodation

- **Budget**: €25–€60 per night for hostel dorms, basic guesthouses, or campsites. Smaller alpine towns away from ski hubs remain affordable year-round.

- **Mid-Range**: €90–€180 per night for 3-star hotels, mid-sized apartments, or family-run chalets. These are widely available in towns like Annecy, Grenoble, and Chamonix.

- **Luxury**: €250–€600+ per night for 5-star resorts, spa hotels, or private chalets with hot tubs and personal chefs. In Courchevel or Méribel, peak-season chalets can surpass €1,000 per night.

Food & Drink

- **Budget meals**: €8–€15 for sandwiches, crêpes, or small plates at casual cafés. Supermarkets also sell ready-made meals for €5–€10.

- **Mid-range dining**: €25–€40 per person for a two-course dinner at a brasserie.

- **Fine dining**: €80–€200+ per person at Michelin-starred restaurants in Annecy, Megève, or Courchevel.
  Drinks range from €3–€5 for coffee or local beer to €5–€10 for a glass of wine in restaurants.

Transport

- **Airport transfers**: €20–€80 per person depending on distance and method (shuttle vs. private car).

- **Train journeys**: €25–€90 depending on distance, time, and whether you book in advance. Paris–Grenoble on TGV averages €50–€70 if purchased ahead.

- **Car rental**: €40–€70 per day for a small car, with higher rates for 4x4s or winter tires. Fuel costs average €1.90–€2.10 per liter.

- **Local transport**: Buses within towns usually cost €1.50–€3 per ride.

Activities

- **Ski passes**: €50–€75 per day in major resorts; weekly passes range from €250–€350. Smaller ski areas can be as low as €25–€40 per day.

- **Equipment rental**: €25–€45 per day for skis, boots, and poles. Snowboards, touring skis, or premium gear cost more.

- **Guided excursions**: Half-day hikes with a guide €30–€50; full-day adventure sports (paragliding, canyoning) €80–€150.

- **Museums & cultural attractions**: €5–€15, with discounts for students, seniors, or families.

Overall Daily Budget Estimates (per person)

- **Backpacker**: €60–€100.

- **Mid-range traveler**: €120–€220.

- **Luxury traveler**: €350–€800+.

4.2 Budget Traveler Hacks & Backpacker Tips

Exploring the French Alps on a budget is not only possible but rewarding. With smart planning, you can experience the grandeur of the mountains without breaking the bank.

Accommodation Strategies

- Stay in **hostels or gîtes d'étape** (simple mountain lodges popular with hikers). Many charge around €25–€40 per night.

- Use **campgrounds** in summer, many of which are located near lakes and cost under €20 per night with your own tent.

- Explore **Couchsurfing** or **Workaway** opportunities for cultural immersion and free lodging.

Food on a Budget

- Shop at supermarkets like Carrefour, Intermarché, or Coop (in Geneva). Pre-made meals, bread, cheese, and charcuterie make for budget-friendly picnics with alpine views.

- Look for **lunchtime menus** in local restaurants. Many brasseries offer two- or three-course specials for €12–€18.

- Bring a reusable water bottle—tap water is safe and excellent throughout the Alps.

Transport Savings

- Use **regional buses and trains** instead of private shuttles. Booking in advance on SNCF often slashes fares by 30–50%.

- Hitchhiking is less common today but still practiced in mountain valleys where locals are used to giving rides.

- For group travel, consider **carpooling apps like BlaBlaCar**, which are affordable and often faster than buses.

Activities on a Shoestring

- Take advantage of free activities: hiking, swimming in alpine lakes, or wandering historic towns.

- Choose smaller ski resorts like Les Gets, La Clusaz, or Vaujany for lower lift pass costs.

- Look for **free cultural events**, particularly in summer when towns host concerts and open-air film screenings.

Backpacker Insider Tip
Bring your student ID—even if you are in your late twenties, many attractions and transport companies still honor international student discounts.

4.3 Mid-Range Traveler Strategies

Mid-range travelers will find the Alps comfortable, with options to balance indulgence and savings.

Smart Accommodation Choices

- Rent **self-catered apartments** or Airbnb-style lodgings. These often cost less than hotels and let you cook your own meals.

- Book family-run hotels or **auberges** in smaller villages rather than staying in marquee resorts.

- Travel in **shoulder seasons** (spring and autumn) for significantly cheaper room rates.

Dining Well Without Overspending

- Mix meals: enjoy a few splurge dinners but rely on casual dining or self-catering most of the time.

- Seek out **mountain huts (refuges)** that serve hearty set meals for €15–€20.

- Take advantage of **regional food markets**, where €10 buys fresh bread, cheese, fruit, and cured meat for a full picnic.

Activities

- Opt for **multi-day ski passes** that reduce per-day costs.

- Join **group tours** instead of private guides for hikes or cultural excursions.

- Try summer activities like kayaking, biking, or climbing via ferrata routes, which cost less than heli-skiing or paragliding.

Insider Tip: Many alpine towns have **tourist cards** included with accommodations. These offer free bus rides, reduced lift tickets, and discounts on museums.

4.4 Luxury Indulgences: Where to Splurge

For luxury seekers, the French Alps are a playground of indulgence. From designer chalets to fine dining and exclusive activities, opportunities abound to experience the Alps at their most glamorous.

Accommodation

- **Private chalets** in Courchevel 1850, Méribel, and Megève come with heated pools, spas, personal chefs, and concierge services. Prices often exceed €1,000 per night during ski season.

- **Luxury hotels** such as Les Airelles in Courchevel or Hotel Mont-Blanc in Chamonix offer Michelin-starred restaurants and award-winning spas.

Fine Dining

The French Alps are home to numerous Michelin-starred restaurants. Annecy, Courchevel, and Megève are particularly renowned for culinary innovation that combines alpine tradition with modern flair. Expect tasting menus from €150–€250 per person.

Exclusive Experiences

- **Heli-skiing** in neighboring Italy or Switzerland, with transfers arranged from French resorts.

- **Private ski instructors** for tailored lessons.

- **Luxury spa treatments** using alpine botanicals or thermal waters.

- **VIP festival experiences**, such as premium seating at Annecy's Fête du Lac fireworks.

Insider Tip : Splurge on one or two big experiences, such as a private helicopter ride over Mont Blanc, and balance with standard accommodation or dining. It creates a memorable highlight without overspending on every detail.

4.5 Saving with Passes, Cards & Off-Season Deals

No matter your budget, smart use of passes and cards can reduce costs considerably.

Transport Passes

- **Carte Avantage Jeune, Famille, or Senior (SNCF)**: Annual discount cards for French trains. They cut fares by up to 30% and pay for themselves after a few journeys.

- **Regional transport passes**: Many alpine towns sell passes covering local buses and ski lifts.

Ski Passes

- Multi-day passes (3, 6, or 7 days) are cheaper per day than single-day tickets.

- Some ski areas offer **family passes** with discounts for groups.

- Consider **smaller ski domains**, which often partner with neighboring resorts for shared lift access at lower prices.

City & Tourist Cards

- **Annecy City Pass** and **Grenoble Alpes Pass** bundle museum entries, public transport, and activity discounts.

- In Chamonix, the **Mont Blanc MultiPass** gives access to lifts, attractions, and buses.

Off-Season Deals

- Visit in May, June, September, or October for up to 40% lower accommodation prices.

- Many ski resorts offer discounted spring passes from mid-March onward when snow is still good.

- Book early: ski season packages offered in the summer often include "early bird" reductions.

Insider Tip : Always ask at your hotel or tourist office about seasonal promotions. Locals are often the first to know about flash sales or community-organized discount programs.

The French Alps can be as affordable or extravagant as you choose. Backpackers can live off fresh bread and cheese while camping in flowered valleys, while luxury travelers can unwind in world-class chalets with panoramic hot tubs. Most visitors fall somewhere in between, carefully choosing when to save and when to splurge. With a clear understanding of costs and smart use of discounts, passes, and timing, you can design an alpine holiday that matches both your budget and your dreams.

Chapter 5: Where to Stay: Villages, Cities & Mountain Retreats

Deciding where to stay in the French Alps is just as important as choosing what to do. The landscapes stretch across multiple regions, each with its own rhythm, scenery, and personality. Whether you want the cozy intimacy of a high-altitude hamlet, the cultural buzz of an Alpine city, or the refined comfort of a ski chalet, your accommodation choice will shape your trip. In 2025–2026, travelers have more options than ever, with eco-lodges, stylish Airbnbs, and new luxury resorts complementing the traditional favorites.

5.1 Charming Alpine Villages

The villages of the French Alps are the heart of the region's identity. Staying here means waking up to mountain views, strolling through narrow lanes, and enjoying local traditions.

- **Chamonix**: Dynamic and international, ideal for adventure seekers.

- **Megève**: Elegant, romantic, and luxurious.

- **Les Gets & Morzine**: Family-friendly with year-round events.

- **Bonneval-sur-Arc**: Traditional, remote, and peaceful.

Price Ranges (per night, 2025–2026):

- Guesthouses & B&Bs: €70–€150

- Mid-range hotels: €120–€250

- Luxury chalets & boutique stays: €300–€700+

Villages are best for couples, families, and cultural travelers who want atmosphere and proximity to hiking or skiing without city distractions.

5.2 Bustling Gateway Cities (Grenoble, Chambéry, Annecy)

For convenience and culture, gateway cities offer museums, nightlife, and better transport links.

- **Grenoble**: Urban energy surrounded by peaks.

- **Chambéry**: Historic charm with Savoie heritage.

- **Annecy**: Romantic canals, boutique shopping, and lakeside leisure.

Price Ranges (per night, 2025–2026):

- Budget hostels & simple hotels: €40–€90

- Mid-range hotels: €100–€180

- Upscale hotels or boutique lakeside stays: €200–€400+

Cities suit digital nomads, budget-conscious travelers, and those who want cultural variety alongside easy transport to surrounding mountains.

5.3 Ski Resorts & Winter Chalets

The French Alps' reputation rests on its legendary ski resorts, from world-famous names to traditional villages.

- **Les Trois Vallées (Courchevel, Méribel, Val Thorens)**: Luxury and variety.

- **Espace Killy (Val d'Isère & Tignes)**: Adventurous skiing and lively après-ski.

- **La Clusaz & Le Grand-Bornand**: Traditional charm and family-friendly.

Chalet & Resort Price Ranges (per night, 2025–2026):

- Budget apartments: €80–€150

- Mid-range hotels & chalets: €180–€300

- Luxury ski-in/ski-out chalets: €500–€1,500+ (with private staff and spa facilities)

Staying in a ski resort is best for winter sports enthusiasts, groups of friends, and luxury seekers. Summer mountain biking and hiking packages are increasingly popular too.

5.4 Lakeside Escapes & Countryside Retreats

For travelers wanting peace, lakeside towns and countryside stays are perfect.

- **Lake Annecy**: Clean, scenic, and active.

- **Lake Geneva (Évian-les-Bains, Thonon-les-Bains)**: Spas and wine country.

- **Countryside Stays**: Vineyards, farmhouses, and eco-retreats.

Price Ranges (per night, 2025–2026):

- Simple farm stays or small guesthouses: €60–€120

- Mid-range lake-view apartments & boutique hotels: €130–€250

- Luxury spa retreats or vineyard stays: €300–€600+

These options are great for wellness seekers, families with young children, and couples who want a calm, romantic environment.

5.5 Accommodation Styles: Hotels, Hostels, Airbnb & Eco-Lodges

Every budget is covered in the Alps, with evolving options for 2025–2026.

- **Hotels**: Ranging from simple inns to five-star resorts.

    - Price: €70–€150 (budget), €180–€350 (mid-range), €400–€800+ (luxury)

- **Hostels**: Modern, social, often with co-working spaces.

    - Price: €25–€50 for dorm beds, €70–€100 for private rooms

- **Airbnb & Vacation Rentals**: Ideal for families and groups.

    - Price: €90–€200 for small apartments, €250–€600+ for entire chalets

- **Eco-Lodges & Sustainable Stays**: Renewable energy, organic food, minimal impact.

  - Price: €120–€250 mid-range, €300–€500+ luxury eco-resorts

- **Luxury Retreats**: Spa hotels, private chalets, lake-view villas.

  - Price: €500–€1,200+ per night depending on exclusivity

Accommodation in the French Alps is as diverse as the mountains themselves. Budget hostels, rustic chalets, boutique hotels, and luxury spas all find their place. By 2025–2026, eco-conscious stays and tech-savvy Airbnbs will only grow, giving travelers even more options. Choose a base that matches your travel style, whether it's the intimacy of a stone village, the cultural energy of a city, or the indulgence of a ski-in chalet, and the Alps will reward you with memories as rich as its landscapes.

Chapter 6: Flagship Destinations & Iconic Attractions

The French Alps are vast, stretching across multiple regions and offering landscapes as diverse as glacial peaks, turquoise lakes, spa towns, and cobblestone villages. Within this mosaic, some destinations stand out as icons: places every traveler should know about, even if their trip leans toward the offbeat. These flagship spots define the region's identity and attract millions of visitors each year. By 2025–2026, they have only grown more dynamic, balancing tradition with innovation. Whether you are planning a winter ski escape, a summer lake holiday, or a cultural city break, the following destinations anchor the Alpine experience.

6.1 Mont Blanc & Chamonix

At 4,810 meters, **Mont Blanc** is Western Europe's highest peak and the undisputed emblem of the Alps. It dominates the skyline, drawing climbers, hikers, and dreamers from around the globe. The surrounding **Chamonix Valley** has built its reputation as the ultimate adventure capital.

Why Visit

Chamonix combines raw mountain drama with a lively town atmosphere. You don't need to be a mountaineer to appreciate it; cable cars, gondolas, and mountain railways provide easy access to unforgettable viewpoints. By 2025, improvements to visitor infrastructure have made access smoother, with timed entries for popular attractions helping reduce crowding.

Highlights

- **Aiguille du Midi Cable Car**: Rising to 3,842 meters, this ride offers panoramic views of Mont Blanc and even the Matterhorn on clear days. A glass-floored platform called "Step into the Void" thrills visitors with its dizzying perspective.

- **Mer de Glace**: France's largest glacier, accessible by the Montenvers Railway. Travelers can enter an ice cave sculpted each year to reveal the glacier's interior.

- **Adventure Sports**: From skiing and snowboarding in winter to paragliding, trail running, and mountain biking in summer, Chamonix sets the pace for adrenaline seekers.

Traveler Tips

- **Best for**: Adventure travelers, photographers, families seeking iconic Alpine sights.

- **When to go**: Winter (December–March) for skiing; summer (June–September) for hiking and climbing.

- **Price snapshot**: Cable car tickets €60–€75 round trip; guided glacier tours €50–€100.

6.2 Annecy: The "Venice of the Alps"

Few Alpine cities capture the imagination like **Annecy**, with its turquoise lake, medieval old town, and pastel-colored houses reflected in canals. It has earned the nickname the "Venice of the Alps," though its beauty is distinctly Alpine.

Why Visit

Annecy balances natural splendor with cultural vibrancy. Lake Annecy is often ranked among the cleanest in Europe, and by 2025, expanded cycling paths and eco-friendly lake ferries have enhanced sustainable tourism.

Highlights

- **Old Town (Vieille Ville)**: Cobblestone lanes, canals, and markets create an irresistible atmosphere. The 12th-century Château d'Annecy now houses a museum on regional history.

- **Lake Annecy**: Swimming, paddleboarding, and boat cruises dominate summer, while winter still charms with mist rising over the water.

- **Festivals**: The Annecy International Animation Film Festival (June) remains the world's leading event in the field, while the Fête du Lac (August) dazzles with fireworks.

Traveler Tips

- **Best for**: Couples, families, culture lovers, wellness seekers.

- **When to go**: Summer (July–August) for lake activities, autumn (September–October) for peaceful walks and wine harvests.

- **Price snapshot**: Bike rentals from €15/day; lake cruises €20–€30; boutique hotel stays €150–€300/night.

6.3 Grenoble: The Capital of the Alps

Nicknamed the "Capital of the Alps," **Grenoble** blends urban sophistication with mountain access. Unlike small Alpine villages, Grenoble is a thriving university and tech hub with a strong cultural identity.

Why Visit

Grenoble's location, surrounded by three mountain ranges, gives it dramatic views from nearly every angle. Yet it is also home to vibrant markets, innovative museums, and a buzzing student population that keeps the city youthful.

Highlights

- **Bastille Fortress & Cable Car**: The iconic bubble-shaped gondolas whisk travelers up to the fortress, where hiking trails and panoramic terraces await.

- **Museums**: The Grenoble Museum of Fine Arts rivals Parisian collections, while the Museum of Resistance and Deportation explores WWII history.

- **Urban Culture**: Street art tours and outdoor cafés give the city a creative, modern edge.

Traveler Tips

- **Best for**: Digital nomads, city lovers, history buffs, foodies.

- **When to go**: Year-round, with lively student activity during spring and autumn.

- **Price snapshot**: Cable car €10 round trip; museum entry €8–€12; hotel rooms €100–€200/night.

6.4 Aix-les-Bains & Lac du Bourget

On the shores of France's largest natural lake, **Aix-les-Bains** offers a completely different Alpine experience. Here, the focus is on relaxation, wellness, and water rather than peaks.

Why Visit

Famous for its thermal baths since Roman times, Aix-les-Bains has reinvented itself as a wellness hub. By 2025, modern spa facilities and eco-certified lake cruises make it attractive for slow travelers.

Highlights

- **Thermal Baths & Spas**: Visitors can enjoy mineral-rich waters at centers like Thermes Chevalley.

- **Lake Activities**: Sailing, fishing, and swimming in Lac du Bourget provide a summer counterpoint to Alpine skiing.

- **Cultural Heritage**: Roman ruins and Belle Époque villas reveal Aix's historic layers.

Traveler Tips

- **Best for**: Wellness seekers, retirees, families with children.

- **When to go**: Spring and summer (May–September) for lake activities, autumn for spa retreats.

- **Price snapshot**: Spa packages from €30–€100; lake cruises €15–€25; mid-range hotels €120–€220/night.

6.5 Megève, Morzine & Other Famous Resorts

The French Alps are studded with world-class resorts, each with its own personality. Among the most renowned are **Megève** and **Morzine**, though countless others compete for attention.

Why Visit

These resorts combine excellent skiing with village charm and high-quality services. By 2025, many have expanded their year-round offerings to include summer mountain biking, festivals, and wellness programs.

Highlights

- **Megève**: Elegant and refined, with luxury shopping, horse-drawn carriages, and Michelin-starred dining. Perfect for upscale travelers.

- **Morzine**: Part of the Portes du Soleil ski area, Morzine attracts families and young skiers. It offers lively après-ski in winter and mountain biking in summer.

- **Other Notables**:

  - **Val d'Isère**: Expert skiing and energetic nightlife.

  - **Courchevel**: Known for ultra-luxury chalets and international celebrity visitors.

  - **Les Deux Alpes**: A glacier resort offering summer skiing.

Traveler Tips

- **Best for**: Skiers, snowboarders, luxury seekers, active families.

- **When to go**: Winter (December–April) for skiing; July–August for biking and festivals.

- **Price snapshot**: Lift passes €60–€75/day; après-ski dinners €30–€80; luxury hotels €400–€1,000/night.

6.6 Suggested Mini Itineraries

Exploring the French Alps can be overwhelming given the sheer variety of landscapes, towns, and activities. To help you make the most of your time, here are sample mini itineraries written in a narrative style. They are designed for travelers with just a day or two in each destination, blending iconic sights with authentic local moments.

Mont Blanc & Chamonix
Begin your morning with the ascent to the Aiguille du Midi, where glass viewing platforms and sweeping views of Mont Blanc put you face-to-face with the high peaks of Europe. After returning to the valley, wander the streets of Chamonix, stopping in mountain outfitters, artisan chocolate shops, and cafés with glacier views. In the afternoon, ride the Montenvers train to the Mer de Glace, then finish your day with a hearty Savoyard dinner of fondue or tartiflette in a traditional chalet restaurant. If time allows the next day, consider a gentle alpine hike such as the Lac Blanc trail, where wildflowers and panoramic vistas offer a softer yet equally stunning side of the massif.

Annecy: The "Venice of the Alps"

Arrive early to enjoy Annecy's canals before the streets fill with visitors. Stroll along the pastel houses of the old town, crossing stone bridges and pausing at the Palais de l'Isle, a 12th-century island castle. Spend midday on the shores of Lake Annecy, either picnicking at Jardins de l'Europe or taking a boat cruise across its turquoise waters. In the afternoon, climb up to the Château d'Annecy for sweeping views over the rooftops, then descend back to town for dinner on a lively terrace serving perch fillets or raclette. On a second day, cycle a section of the lakeside path, stopping in small villages and swimming spots along the way.

Grenoble: The Capital of the Alps

Start your exploration with a cable car ride up to the Bastille fortress, where panoramic views stretch across the city and the encircling mountains. Return to the center to walk Grenoble's pedestrian squares, including Place Saint-André with its Gothic parliament building. The afternoon is well spent at the Musée de Grenoble, home to both old masters and modern works. Coffee in a student-filled café gives you a taste of Grenoble's youthful energy. If staying longer, explore the riverside paths or take a short tram ride to the nearby Parc Paul Mistral for an easygoing outdoor escape. Evening dining in Grenoble offers everything from

73

traditional Dauphinois dishes to inventive modern cuisine.

Aix-les-Bains & Lac du Bourget

Morning is best spent on the waterfront of France's largest natural lake. Take a leisurely stroll along the esplanade, watching sailboats glide across the blue surface. A boat excursion offers a different perspective, leading you to secluded coves and views of the abbey of Hautecombe perched on the shore. After lunch in a lakeside bistro, consider a thermal spa session in Aix-les-Bains, the town long famed for its restorative waters. The late afternoon invites exploration of Belle Époque villas and leafy boulevards, followed by dinner paired with wines from nearby Savoie vineyards. Those with an extra day can venture into the surrounding hills for hikes overlooking Lac du Bourget, combining alpine air with the serenity of water views.

Megève, Morzine & Other Famous Resorts

In Megève, start with a stroll through the cobblestone streets, where horse-drawn carriages and chic boutiques create an elegant alpine charm. Spend midday on the slopes in winter or on walking trails in summer, then relax in a stylish après-ski lounge or spa. Morzine, by contrast, offers a more active and family-oriented rhythm: mornings on mountain bikes or ski runs, afternoons by the outdoor pool or skating rink, and evenings filled with casual meals of crêpes or wood-fired pizza. Smaller resorts like Les Gets or Avoriaz each have their own flavor, whether it is architecture blending with cliffs or lively festivals that animate the villages. With two days, you can mix relaxation and adventure, experiencing both the luxury touches and the approachable alpine culture that make these resorts timeless favorites.

The flagship destinations of the French Alps are not just stops on an itinerary but defining experiences. Mont Blanc inspires awe, Annecy charms with its canals, Grenoble energizes with culture, Aix-les-Bains soothes with its waters, and the great resorts deliver world-class skiing. Together they represent the essence of the Alps in 2025–2026: a region that embraces adventure and relaxation, tradition and innovation, nature and culture.

Chapter 7: Hidden Gems & Off-the-Beaten-Path Adventures

The French Alps are celebrated for world-famous resorts, glittering lakes, and well-trodden peaks. Yet beyond the flagship destinations lies another side of the region—quiet valleys where life still revolves around local rhythms, forgotten fortresses guarding mountain passes, and trails where you are more likely to encounter marmots than crowds. For travelers in 2025–2026, when sustainability and authenticity are increasingly shaping trip choices, these hidden corners provide a chance to slow down, connect deeply, and experience the Alps as locals do.

7.1 Secret Villages & Untouched Valleys

While Chamonix and Annecy receive global attention, smaller alpine villages remain remarkably unspoiled. In Haute-Savoie, the hamlet of Sixt-Fer-à-Cheval rests at the entrance to a horseshoe-shaped cirque lined with waterfalls. Life here feels suspended in time, with wooden chalets, traditional inns, and trails leading into nature reserves. It is ideal for those seeking peace after time in bustling resorts.

Further south, the Ubaye Valley near Barcelonnette blends French alpine charm with a surprising Mexican influence, the legacy of 19th-century emigrants who returned with colorful villas and recipes. Few international visitors make the journey, but those who do enjoy river rafting in summer and quiet ski stations in winter.

The Beaufortain Valley, known for its namesake cheese, is another rewarding detour. Rolling pastures framed by jagged peaks create postcard-worthy scenery, while working farms welcome travelers curious about traditional production methods. Staying in Beaufort village offers a gentle pace of life, where evenings are spent sampling tomme cheese with a glass of local Mondeuse wine.

For families, these valleys offer space for children to play freely and safe, easy hikes. For couples or solo travelers, the draw lies in serenity and cultural richness away from mass tourism.

7.2 Remote Hiking Trails & Natural Parks

The French Alps are crisscrossed with some of Europe's finest trails, and beyond the popular GR routes are countless less-traveled paths. In the Chartreuse Regional Natural Park, trails wind through dense forests and limestone cliffs, leading to caves and hidden monasteries where monks still produce the famous Chartreuse liqueur. The landscape is rugged but the routes are manageable for intermediate hikers, making it an excellent alternative to the busier Mont Blanc circuit.

Another overlooked gem is the Vanoise National Park in Savoie. Though established as France's first national park in 1963, it remains less crowded than the adjacent Italian Gran Paradiso. Here, ibex roam freely, alpine lakes shimmer beneath high passes, and multi-day treks connect rustic refuges where evenings are spent sharing meals with fellow hikers.

For those wanting something more meditative, the Queyras Regional Natural Park in the southern Alps offers light-filled valleys with stone villages and chapels decorated in vivid frescoes. Trails are gentle compared to the north, making it perfect for slow travelers or those looking for an accessible introduction to alpine hiking.

Travelers in 2025 are also taking to new eco-marked routes designed to highlight biodiversity. Some follow pollinator corridors, where wildflower meadows support bees and butterflies, while others are themed around heritage, linking old shepherds' huts and dry-stone walls. Apps now allow hikers to download trail maps, track elevation gains, and even listen to local oral histories, adding new dimensions to these remote journeys.

7.3 Alpine Heritage Towns Less Visited

While Grenoble and Annecy dominate headlines, lesser-known towns in the Alps reveal the region's layered history. Briançon, perched high in the Hautes-Alpes, is a UNESCO-listed fortified town with star-shaped ramparts designed by Vauban. Narrow lanes lead to small cafés and artisan shops, while its elevated position provides sweeping views.

In Maurienne Valley, Saint-Jean-de-Maurienne carries a quieter character but is celebrated as the birthplace of the Opinel knife. Museums tell the story of alpine crafts, and the town serves as a base for cycling routes that challenge even seasoned riders.

Closer to Switzerland, Thonon-les-Bains on Lake Geneva has the grace of a spa town without the heavy crowds. Its lakeside promenades, thermal baths, and medieval chateau offer a gentler, more restorative experience.

These towns are ideal for cultural explorers and history lovers who want to understand how the Alps have long been shaped not only by nature but also by trade, craftsmanship, and strategic geography.

7.4 Unique Local Experiences & Farm Visits

Beyond landscapes and monuments, the French Alps offer immersive local experiences that anchor travelers in daily life. In Savoie and Haute-Savoie, visitors can join guided tours of working dairy farms, where herds of Tarine cows graze on high-altitude pastures. Watching traditional cheese-making and tasting Beaufort or Reblochon fresh from the cellar connects travelers to centuries-old practices.

In the Drôme region at the foot of the Alps, lavender fields and bee farms welcome visitors in summer. Learning about honey production or distilling lavender oil adds sensory depth to the trip. In winter, truffle hunting excursions take place in oak groves with trained dogs, offering a unique seasonal highlight.

Craft traditions also thrive in smaller workshops. In alpine towns such as Albertville, woodcarvers and potters open their studios, while in the Tarentaise Valley, cheesemakers run short apprenticeships for curious travelers. These experiences are not tourist shows but genuine exchanges, often led by families who have preserved knowledge for generations.

For food lovers, farm-to-table dinners are on the rise in 2025–2026. Hosted in converted barns or chalets, they feature seasonal menus paired with local wines. Guests often dine communally, creating bonds with fellow travelers and hosts alike. For families, these encounters are both educational and fun, teaching children where their food comes from in interactive ways.

7.5 Future Hotspots for 2026

As tourism patterns shift, new areas of the French Alps are gaining attention. One is the Bauges Massif, located between Annecy and Chambéry. Long overshadowed by its glamorous neighbors, the Bauges has been designated a UNESCO Global Geopark for its unique geology and sustainable initiatives. In 2026, new eco-lodges and cycling routes are expected to attract travelers looking for a balance of comfort and conservation.

The Southern Alps around Sisteron and Gap are also emerging as adventure hubs. Improved transport links and the rise of outdoor sports—from paragliding to canyoning—are drawing younger travelers and digital nomads. Smaller ski stations here are promoting four-season tourism, with trail running, mountain biking, and wellness retreats filling the calendar beyond winter.

Another trend to watch is the rise of agritourism villages where visitors stay on working farms. Pilot projects in the Tarentaise and Queyras valleys are offering immersive week-long stays where travelers share daily chores, cook with hosts, and learn sustainable land practices. These programs are expected to grow in 2026 as more visitors seek meaningful, slow-travel experiences.

Finally, advances in rail connectivity mean that towns once considered remote are now weekend-accessible from Paris or Geneva. As the Alpine region adapts to climate change and shifts in visitor demand, travelers can expect a more diversified tourism landscape—one that prioritizes local culture, environmental stewardship, and year-round accessibility.

Chapter 8: Outdoor Adventures Year-Round

The French Alps are an adventure playground in every season, with landscapes that change dramatically between snow-covered winters, flower-strewn springs, sunlit summers, and golden autumns. While skiing remains the region's global calling card, travelers in 2025–2026 are increasingly seeking variety: summer treks across high passes, paragliding above turquoise lakes, or unwinding in thermal spas. Whether you are a thrill-seeker, a family looking for gentle outdoor fun, or a wellness traveler in search of restorative escapes, the Alps offer an experience tailored to every rhythm.

8.1 Skiing & Snowboarding

For most visitors, skiing is the quintessential alpine activity, and the French Alps remain unrivaled in scale and variety. Mega-resorts such as Les Trois Vallées, Paradiski, and Espace Killy offer hundreds of interconnected kilometers of pistes, with runs suited to complete beginners and seasoned experts. Resorts like Méribel or Val d'Isère have invested in new high-speed lifts and eco-friendly snowmaking systems, ensuring reliability and sustainability for 2025–2026.

Snowboarders continue to favor Avoriaz and Les Deux Alpes for their terrain parks, halfpipes, and freeride zones. Meanwhile, smaller stations like La Clusaz or Les Gets appeal to families and budget-conscious travelers, offering intimate slopes, shorter lift queues, and friendly ski schools.

Off-piste skiing and ski touring are increasingly popular, especially in Chamonix and La Grave, where guides lead small groups into untouched powder fields. Safety has become a major focus, with avalanche training sessions and digital apps providing real-time snow condition updates. Travelers should expect ski pass prices ranging from €50 to €70 per day in major resorts, though family packages and multi-day deals reduce costs.

Equipment rentals typically add €30 to €40 per day.

For non-skiers, many resorts now feature snowshoe trails, winter hiking, and even dog sledding, ensuring that everyone can enjoy the alpine winter atmosphere.

8.2 Hiking, Trekking & Via Ferrata

As the snow melts, the Alps reveal a vast network of hiking routes that attract walkers of all levels. Day hikers can enjoy accessible trails around Lake Annecy, such as the climb to Mont Veyrier, which rewards with sweeping lake views. Families often favor paths in the Bauges or Chartreuse ranges, where trails meander through forests and meadows without extreme elevation gain.

For multi-day trekkers, the Tour du Mont Blanc remains the region's most famous circuit, circling Europe's highest peak across France, Italy, and Switzerland. While popular, it can be tailored to quieter sections or shorter itineraries. The GR5 trail, running from Lake Geneva to the Mediterranean, offers another epic challenge, with hikers completing sections over weeks or tackling weekend portions.

A unique alpine experience is the via ferrata—protected climbing routes fitted with cables, ladders, and bridges. Originating during World War I in the Dolomites, via ferrata routes are now widespread across the French Alps. They allow adventurers to scale cliff faces and traverse ridges with relative safety, though harnesses, helmets, and a guide are strongly recommended. Prices for guided via ferrata sessions typically range from €50 to €80 per person.

Digital tools are making hiking easier in 2025–2026, with apps like Visorando and AllTrails offering GPS tracks and offline maps. Many regions are also improving waymarking and building eco-refuges, giving trekkers sustainable options for overnight stays.

8.3 Lakes, Water Sports & Swimming

Summer in the Alps is synonymous with lakeside relaxation and water sports. Lake Annecy is the star, famous for its crystal-clear waters fed by mountain springs. Families flock to grassy beaches such as Talloires or Albigny, where lifeguards ensure safe swimming. Kayak and paddleboard rentals (€10–€20 per hour) let visitors explore at their own pace, while boat cruises reveal hidden coves.

Lake Geneva (Lac Léman) offers a more cosmopolitan vibe, with towns like Thonon-les-Bains and Évian combining beach clubs, thermal spas, and sailing. The smaller but no less beautiful Lac du Bourget near Aix-les-Bains is favored for tranquility and less-crowded shores.

Adventurers seeking thrills can try canyoning in mountain gorges, where guides lead groups through waterfalls and rock slides using ropes and natural pools. White-water rafting is another highlight, particularly in the Ubaye and Isère rivers, with trips ranging from family-friendly floats to adrenaline-packed rapids. Expect prices from €40 to €70 per person depending on route difficulty and duration.

For those looking for serenity, alpine tarns such as Lac Blanc above Chamonix offer peaceful swims and picnic spots framed by jagged peaks. These smaller lakes, reached only by foot, feel worlds away from the busier tourist centers.

8.4 Paragliding, Cycling & Rock Climbing

Few experiences capture the grandeur of the Alps like paragliding. Annecy is one of Europe's most famous take-off points, with pilots soaring above the turquoise lake and patchwork valleys. Tandem flights, accessible even to first-timers, last 20 to 40 minutes and cost between €100 and €150. Other hotspots include Chamonix, where flights glide past glaciers, and the Chartreuse, known for gentler thermals.

Cycling is another alpine passion, with routes for both road cyclists and mountain bikers. Road cyclists can tackle legendary Tour de France climbs such as Alpe d'Huez, Col du Galibier, or Col de la Madeleine. These ascents are grueling but iconic, drawing enthusiasts from around the world. Mountain bikers, meanwhile, flock to resorts like Les Gets and Morzine, which transform ski lifts into bike lifts each summer, granting access to downhill trails and enduro tracks. Bike rentals typically cost €50 to €90 per day, with guided tours available.

Rock climbing thrives across the Alps, from beginner-friendly crags in the Aravis to the towering limestone cliffs of the Vercors. Chamonix attracts expert alpinists with multi-pitch routes on granite spires, while families can join half-day climbing sessions on bolted walls. Indoor climbing gyms in cities like Grenoble provide year-round practice opportunities. Guided climbing excursions start around €60 per person.

These sports appeal to different traveler types: couples often choose tandem paragliding as a romantic experience, while families lean toward beginner bike routes or guided climbs. Digital nomads, on the other hand, often balance workdays with outdoor adrenaline sessions, making activities like paragliding or cycling an attractive break.

8.5 Wellness & Thermal Spas

Adventure in the Alps is not only about high-energy sports; it also includes rest, recovery, and well-being. The region has been a hub for thermal spas since Roman times, and in 2025–2026, wellness tourism is stronger than ever.

Aix-les-Bains, on the shores of Lac du Bourget, remains the premier spa destination, with thermal waters believed to soothe joints and muscles. Évian-les-Bains and Thonon-les-Bains on Lake Geneva offer luxurious wellness centers where treatments combine hydrotherapy with modern techniques such as cryotherapy or aromatherapy.

Smaller mountain towns have developed boutique wellness retreats, often in eco-lodges where programs combine yoga, meditation, and spa therapies with local organic cuisine. Some retreats focus on "alpine mindfulness," encouraging participants to connect with nature through guided forest walks and breathing exercises.

Prices vary widely: entry to public thermal baths costs around €20 to €30, while full spa packages at luxury hotels can exceed €200. Families often choose budget-friendly pools with heated outdoor areas, while couples and solo travelers may indulge in high-end resorts.

Wellness is also linked to recovery from active sports. Many ski resorts now feature wellness centers, ensuring tired muscles find relief after days on the slopes. Increasingly, travelers combine adventure and relaxation in the same trip—rafting one day, spa therapy the next—creating a balanced alpine escape.

Chapter 9: Culinary Delights of the French Alps

Food in the French Alps is more than sustenance—it is culture, heritage, and comfort rolled into every dish. Born from centuries of mountain life, Alpine cuisine is hearty and ingenious, shaped by long winters, local produce, and a deep sense of community. When you travel here, eating is not just dining; it is sharing in a tradition that blends rustic simplicity with gourmet innovation. In this chapter, we explore the flavors that define the French Alps, from classic mountain meals to high-end gastronomy, from bustling local markets to après-ski celebrations.

9.1 Traditional Alpine Dishes (Fondue, Raclette, Tartiflette)

The backbone of Alpine cuisine rests on simple, filling dishes designed to nourish families through cold nights and long days on the slopes. Cheese is at the center of it all, with Savoie and Haute-Savoie among the richest dairy-producing regions in France.

Fondue Savoyarde is arguably the most iconic dish. It involves melting a blend of cheeses—often Beaufort, Comté, and Tomme de Savoie—with white wine and garlic in a communal pot. Diners spear chunks of bread with long forks and dip them into the bubbling mixture, a ritual that is both social and indulgent. Fondue is traditionally accompanied by charcuterie and a crisp white wine such as Apremont.

Raclette is equally famous, named after the semi-hard cheese that is heated and scraped over boiled potatoes, pickles, and cured meats. The word "racler" means "to scrape," and the dish perfectly embodies Alpine conviviality. Modern raclette grills are often found in chalets and restaurants, allowing groups to melt slices of cheese at the table.

Tartiflette, a relatively modern invention dating back to the 1980s, has quickly become a regional staple. Made with layers of potatoes, lardons, onions, cream, and Reblochon cheese, it is the very definition of comfort food. Its warmth and richness are a perfect end to a day on the slopes.

Other regional specialties include **diots** (smoked Savoyard sausages often served in white wine sauce), **crozets** (small buckwheat pasta squares often baked in gratins), and **farçon**, a sweet-savory pudding of potatoes, dried fruit, and bacon. Desserts are simpler but satisfying: blueberry tarts, chestnut cakes, or bugnes, a kind of fried pastry.

These dishes are not just meals; they are the taste of Alpine resilience and hospitality, a way to gather around the table and celebrate local produce.

9.2 Farm-to-Table & Mountain Markets

The French Alps are dotted with small farms, artisanal producers, and weekly markets that connect travelers directly to the land. Unlike supermarket shopping, Alpine markets are lively gatherings where locals chat, producers proudly display their goods, and travelers discover seasonal specialties.

Markets are typically held once or twice a week in most towns. In Annecy, the Old Town transforms into a vibrant open-air market where stalls overflow with local cheeses, cured meats, fresh vegetables, honey, jams, and handmade crafts. In Chamonix, Friday markets bring together regional producers offering everything from mountain herbs to wildflower honey. Aix-les-Bains and Grenoble have equally celebrated markets, each showcasing the area's terroir.

Cheese lovers should look for **Reblochon, Beaufort, Abondance, and Tomme de Savoie**. Farmers often sell directly at stalls, and tasting before buying is encouraged. Charcuterie is another highlight, particularly cured ham and saucisson flavored with mountain herbs.

Seasonal produce reflects the Alpine cycle. Spring brings wild asparagus, mushrooms, and leafy greens. Summer fills markets with berries, cherries, and peaches. Autumn is a time of chestnuts, apples, and walnuts, while winter emphasizes storage crops like potatoes, pumpkins, and cabbages.

Farm-to-table restaurants in villages like Les Gets and Samoëns highlight this bounty. Many chefs source ingredients from nearby farms, creating menus that change with the seasons. Visiting a market and then enjoying a meal at a local auberge ties together the Alpine experience—freshness, authenticity, and sustainability.

9.3 Michelin-Star Dining & Gourmet Experiences

While rustic meals define Alpine culture, the region is also home to some of France's most creative chefs. Over the last decades, Savoie and Haute-Savoie have attracted culinary innovators who reinterpret mountain traditions into gourmet art. This duality—comfort food and haute cuisine—makes the French Alps a unique gastronomic destination.

In **Megève**, establishments like Flocons de Sel (3 Michelin stars) elevate local ingredients to fine dining masterpieces. Chef Emmanuel Renaut is renowned for blending Alpine herbs, lake fish, and seasonal vegetables into refined dishes that remain deeply rooted in the land.

Annecy boasts the celebrated restaurant of Marc Veyrat, long a pioneer of mountain gastronomy. Known for his use of wild plants, flowers, and herbs foraged from the Alpine landscape, Veyrat has redefined what it means to cook locally.

In **Chamonix**, Michelin-starred dining coexists with casual bistros, offering travelers both indulgent tasting menus and hearty fare. Grenoble and Chambéry also host gourmet spots where chefs balance innovation with tradition.

Beyond Michelin stars, gourmet experiences include truffle tastings, vineyard-to-table pairings, and multi-course meals featuring lake fish, game meats, and artisan cheeses. These dining options remind visitors that the Alps are not only about rustic charm but also about culinary excellence at the highest level.

9.4 Après-Ski Bars, Nightlife & Breweries

Après-ski is an Alpine institution. Once the skis come off, the mountains come alive with music, drinks, and conviviality. Each resort has its own take on this social ritual, ranging from laid-back wine bars to lively clubs.

In **Chamonix**, après-ski begins in cozy pubs and evolves into energetic nightlife. Bars like Chambre Neuf are famous for live bands, while microbreweries such as Micro Brasserie de Chamonix serve craft beers brewed on-site.

Morzine and **Les Deux Alpes** offer a younger, party-oriented scene, with terrace bars filling in the late afternoon and DJ sets lasting into the night. For travelers seeking something quieter, Megève's wine bars and cocktail lounges provide a refined alternative, perfect for couples or groups of friends.

Breweries have gained popularity in recent years, often producing beers infused with Alpine botanicals or honey. Craft cider is also on the rise, pairing beautifully with cheese-heavy dishes. Après-ski is not only about alcohol—many resorts also feature hot chocolate bars, tea houses, and crêperies for families and non-drinkers.

9.5 Local Wines & Spirits of Savoie & Haute-Savoie

The French Alps are home to a distinctive wine tradition, largely unknown outside the region but increasingly celebrated for its quality. The vineyards of Savoie and Haute-Savoie produce crisp, aromatic whites and light reds perfectly suited to local cuisine.

Among whites, **Jacquère** is the most widely planted grape, producing refreshing wines often paired with fondue or raclette. **Altesse (Roussette de Savoie)** yields more structured wines with notes of pear and almond, while **Chasselas**, common around Lake Geneva, is elegant and easy-drinking. **Roussanne (Bergeron)** produces rich, age-worthy whites, often described as the jewels of Savoie.

Red wines, though less dominant, include **Mondeuse**, a peppery grape with deep color and lively acidity. Gamay and Pinot Noir are also grown, often resulting in light, fruity wines perfect for summer meals.

Local spirits are equally intriguing. **Génépi**, a herbal liqueur made from mountain wormwood, is the quintessential Alpine digestif, often homemade by families or sold in artisanal shops. **Chartreuse**, crafted by Carthusian monks near Grenoble since the 18th century, remains one of France's most complex and iconic liqueurs, available in green or yellow versions with dozens of herbal ingredients.

These beverages are not just accompaniments to meals; they are cultural expressions of the Alpine environment, bottled traditions that connect visitors to centuries of craftsmanship.

9.6 Traveler's Tips: Dining Costs & Practical Advice

Understanding what to budget for meals in the French Alps helps travelers plan their culinary adventures without surprises. Dining costs can vary widely depending on whether you are in a village auberge, a ski resort, or a Michelin-starred restaurant. Here is what to expect in 2025–2026:

Budget Dining (€8–€20 per person)

- Bakeries and cafés offer sandwiches, quiches, or croque-monsieur for around €6–€10.

- Casual crêperies serve savory galettes or sweet crêpes for €8–€12.

- Market stalls often have cheese-and-charcuterie plates, or sausage and potatoes for under €15.

- A budget-friendly fondue menu in a rustic chalet can start at around €18 per person (shared).

Mid-Range Dining (€25–€50 per person)

- Traditional Alpine restaurants often serve raclette or tartiflette menus with salad and dessert for €25–€35.

- Farm-to-table bistros with seasonal menus usually charge €30–€45 for three courses.

- Après-ski bars with hearty mains (burgers, mountain stews, pizzas) are around €18–€25.

- Local wines by the glass cost €4–€6; a bottle at dinner ranges from €20–€40.

High-End & Gourmet Dining (€70–€200+ per person)

- Michelin-starred tasting menus begin around €85 per person for lunch and can exceed €200 per person for elaborate evening menus.

- Wine pairings add €40–€120 depending on the prestige of the bottles.

- Luxury resorts often bundle multi-course dinners into half-board packages, making gourmet dining slightly more accessible.

Après-Ski & Nightlife Costs

- Draft beer in a mountain pub: €6–€8.

- Craft beers or cocktails: €8–€12.

- Génépi shots or Chartreuse liqueur: €4–€6.

- Live music bars or late-night clubs sometimes charge a small entry fee (€5–€10), but most après-ski spots remain free to enter.

Money-Saving Tips

- Look for lunch menus ("formule déjeuner") at mid-range restaurants; they are often 30–40% cheaper than dinner.

- Shop at village markets to assemble a picnic of cheese, bread, and fruit for under €10 per person.

- Choose family-run auberges in smaller villages—meals are both authentic and more affordable than in big resorts.

- If staying in Airbnb or chalet rentals, try cooking with fresh market ingredients at least once to balance out dining costs.

The culinary landscape of the French Alps is a journey in itself. From the shared warmth of a fondue pot to the precision of a Michelin-starred plate, from bustling markets to late-night après-ski celebrations, every bite and sip tells a story of mountain life. For travelers in 2025–2026, exploring this region's food is not an optional activity—it is an essential way to understand its soul. Whether you are savoring cheese by a fireplace, sampling wines in a vineyard, or raising a glass of génépi under the stars, Alpine cuisine invites you to taste the richness of place, history, and tradition.

Chapter 10: Culture, Traditions & Festivals

The French Alps are not only a playground for skiers, hikers, and adventure seekers—they are also a living cultural landscape. Alpine communities have held on to their unique traditions while also welcoming global influences, resulting in a calendar packed with festivals, celebrations, and artistic expressions. Travelers who take time to dive into local heritage will discover that the mountains tell stories not only through landscapes but also through music, costume, craft, and seasonal rituals.

10.1 Alpine Folklore & Heritage

The cultural identity of the French Alps has been shaped by centuries of life in the mountains. Local traditions often tie directly to the rhythm of the seasons, agricultural cycles, and the challenges of mountain living.

In villages across Savoie and Haute-Savoie, folklore is preserved through oral storytelling, songs, and dances passed down through generations. Tales of shepherds, mountain spirits, and legendary figures such as the "dahu"—a mythical creature said to roam steep Alpine slopes—still echo in children's games and community folklore events.

Architecture reflects this heritage as well. Wooden chalets with overhanging roofs, designed to resist heavy snowfall, are more than picturesque—they are symbols of resilience. Stone barns known as "mazots" once protected harvests and valuables, and many are now restored as guesthouses or cultural landmarks.Travelers can explore Alpine heritage at institutions like the Musée Savoisien in Chambéry, or the Musée Alpin in Chamonix, which illustrate daily life in the mountains. Many towns also maintain open-air museums where old tools, textiles, and costumes are displayed to showcase the Alpine way of life.

Heritage is not locked in the past. Villagers still celebrate transhumance festivals each spring and autumn when herds move between valleys and high pastures. These processions, often with cows adorned in flower garlands and bells, are among the most photogenic and authentic traditions travelers can witness.

10.2 Music, Film & Art Festivals

The French Alps host a surprisingly wide range of cultural festivals, often blending natural settings with artistic expression.

Music festivals take advantage of open-air stages with dramatic mountain backdrops. The Musilac Festival on the shores of Lake Bourget in Aix-les-Bains draws international rock and pop acts each July, while the Au Bonheur des Mômes festival in Le Grand-Bornand specializes in children's performances, making it ideal for families. Classical and jazz lovers will appreciate the Annecy Classic Festival and Jazz à Vienne, which although slightly outside the Alpine core, attract audiences from across Europe.

Film culture also thrives here. The Annecy International Animation Festival is the world's leading event for animated cinema, bringing together creators and fans each June. The Les Arcs Film Festival, held in December in the Tarentaise Valley, focuses on European cinema and is a chic meeting point for filmmakers and moviegoers.

Art festivals showcase contemporary creativity with a mountain twist. Land-art projects and sculpture trails, such as the Biennale of Contemporary Art in Annecy, merge nature with art installations. Villages sometimes host smaller arts and crafts fairs where visitors can meet potters, woodcarvers, and painters who interpret the Alpine landscape through their craft.

These events attract diverse audiences, from young festivalgoers chasing music lineups to families seeking cultural outings, proving that the Alps are as much a cultural stage as a natural one.

10.3 Christmas Markets & Winter Celebrations

Winter in the French Alps carries an almost storybook quality, and Christmas markets heighten the atmosphere. Cities like Annecy, Grenoble, and Chambéry transform their old towns into glowing villages of wooden chalets selling mulled wine, artisanal gifts, and regional treats like gingerbread and spiced nuts. Ice rinks are often set up in central squares, and choirs perform traditional carols.

In mountain resorts such as Megève and Chamonix, the markets are smaller but more intimate, with local artisans selling handmade ornaments, cheeses, and cured meats. Travelers will also notice Alpine touches, like fondue stands and stalls selling génépi, the herbal liqueur of the region.

New Year's Eve is another highlight. Resorts such as Val d'Isère and Les Deux Alpes organize torchlit descents by ski instructors, followed by fireworks displays against snowy peaks. In villages, celebrations are more intimate, with families gathering for festive meals and community dances.

For those visiting in early January, the Epiphany brings another culinary tradition: the galette des rois, a flaky pastry filled with almond cream, enjoyed across France but with regional Alpine variations.

10.4 Summer Events: Outdoor Concerts & Fêtes

Summer in the Alps has a lighter, more communal cultural rhythm. Warm evenings and longer days invite gatherings in village squares, meadows, and lakeshores.

Local **fêtes de village** often center around music, food, and dance. Travelers may stumble upon accordion players leading communal dances, children's games, or contests of traditional sports such as pétanque. These fêtes usually coincide with a saint's day or a seasonal milestone and are excellent opportunities to meet locals.

Open-air concerts are frequent, often free or low-cost. Annecy hosts lakeside performances, while smaller towns organize choral events in churches or parks. Travelers visiting in July will encounter Bastille Day (14 July), marked with fireworks, parades, and community dinners in towns large and small.

Another beloved summer event is the Fête de l'Alpage, celebrated in high pastures with music, cheese tastings, and demonstrations of traditional crafts like butter churning or woodcarving. These gatherings offer a vivid look into Alpine rural life.

10.5 Crafts, Costumes & Local Pride

The French Alps take pride in their crafts, many of which remain deeply tied to agricultural life. Woodcarving, basket weaving, and textile production are still practiced, and village shops often sell handmade items as souvenirs. Cowbells, carved walking sticks, and woven woolen goods carry a distinct Alpine identity.

Costumes remain an important cultural marker. At festivals and heritage events, women often wear embroidered blouses, aprons, and distinctive headpieces, while men don traditional wool trousers, sashes, and hats. These outfits are not costumes in the tourist sense but are symbols of community pride and continuity.

Cheese production is also a form of cultural craftsmanship. Travelers visiting cooperatives or farms can watch how wheels of Beaufort, Tomme de Savoie, or Reblochon are made, often using methods unchanged for centuries. Sampling cheeses alongside local wines ties food directly to cultural identity.

In recent years, younger generations have renewed interest in these traditions, blending them with modern creativity. Festivals now showcase DJs alongside folk dancers, and artisanal products are marketed to global travelers. This combination of old and new ensures that Alpine pride is not static but evolving.

10.6 Suggested Mini Itineraries for Cultural Travelers

A Winter Wonderland of Markets and Traditions (December in Annecy & Chamonix)

Begin your trip in **Annecy**, where the medieval old town glows with Christmas lights and wooden chalets spill aromas of roasted chestnuts and mulled wine. Spend your first evening browsing local crafts and sipping hot chocolate along the canals. The next day, head to **Chamonix**, where the snow-capped Mont Blanc backdrop transforms the market into something magical. End your evening with a torchlit descent show on the slopes followed by a festive raclette dinner in a chalet restaurant.

Summer Festival Escape (July in Aix-les-Bains & Lake Bourget)

Start your morning on the shores of **Lake Bourget**, with a swim or boat ride to appreciate the scenery before the crowds arrive. In the afternoon, wander into **Aix-les-Bains**, where the **Musilac Festival** brings major artists to an open-air lakeside stage. Between sets, sample local Savoie wines at nearby bars or enjoy casual dining in bistros buzzing with festivalgoers.

Your cultural immersion continues the next day with a more traditional village fête in the surrounding countryside, where families gather for music, dancing, and farm-fresh food.

Heritage & Folklore Weekend (Spring in the Villages of Haute-Savoie)

Base yourself in a charming Alpine village such as **Le Grand-Bornand** or **Samoëns** during the **transhumance festivals**. Wake up to the sound of cowbells as herds adorned with flowers parade through cobbled streets. Take part in tastings of local cheeses like Reblochon and Tomme, while folk groups perform dances in traditional costume. Spend your second day hiking a scenic valley, stopping at a farm for a hands-on workshop in butter churning or woodcarving, connecting directly with Alpine heritage.

Art & Film Enthusiast's Escape (June in Annecy)

For culture seekers with a modern edge, time your trip with the **Annecy International Animation Festival**. Your mornings can be spent by the lake or exploring the old town's canals, while afternoons are dedicated to screenings, exhibitions, and panel discussions with global filmmakers. In the evening, join festivalgoers for open-air film screenings projected against the mountain backdrop.

Traveler Tips: Experiencing Culture Like a Local

- **Costs**: Many festivals and village fêtes are free, but expect €10–€30 for entry to concerts or art exhibitions. A mulled wine at a Christmas market costs around €3–€5, while a festive meal during events ranges from €20–€40 per person in local restaurants.

- **Timing**: Always check local calendars in advance; smaller festivals may change dates slightly each year. Booking accommodation early is crucial during peak events like the Annecy Animation Festival or Christmas week.

- **Participation**: Don't just watch—join in. Try the traditional dances, sample regional specialties, or learn a few local phrases to connect with residents.

- **Family-Friendly**: Many events, especially summer fêtes and Christmas markets, are perfect for children, with rides, puppet shows, and games.

Chapter 11: Day Trips & Regional Excursions

The Alps reward travelers with endless discovery, but sometimes the best way to deepen your trip is by stepping beyond your base and exploring the cultural and natural treasures nearby. From Swiss lakeshores to Italian piazzas and Provençal lavender fields, the surrounding regions offer unforgettable contrasts to Alpine landscapes. Whether you are craving cosmopolitan energy, vineyard strolls, or rustic hiking trails across borders, these excursions expand your journey in surprising and enriching ways.

11.1 Geneva & Lake Geneva

Why Go:
A day trip to Geneva opens a window onto
international diplomacy, cosmopolitan living, and
the sparkling shores of one of Europe's largest
lakes. Just a short train or bus ride from many
French Alpine towns, Geneva feels both worldly and
relaxed.

Highlights:

- **The Jet d'Eau:** Geneva's iconic fountain
  shoots water 140 meters into the air, an
  unmissable landmark.

- **Old Town:** Wander cobblestone lanes lined
  with cafés, antique shops, and landmarks
  like St. Peter's Cathedral.

- **The United Nations Office:** Book a
  guided tour to see the Assembly Hall and
  learn about Geneva's role in global politics.

- **Lake Cruises:** From one-hour sightseeing
  loops to half-day journeys toward Montreux,
  the lake offers panoramic views of the Jura
  Mountains and Alpine peaks.

Cultural Touch:
Geneva is multilingual and multicultural, with a vibrant food scene reflecting global communities. Sample fondue at a lakeside brasserie or try international cuisine in the Paquis district.

Traveler Tips:

- **Transport:** From Annecy or Chamonix, buses and trains take 1–2 hours. Tickets cost €15–30 one-way.

- **Budget:** City attractions like the Old Town are free, but UN tours (€15) and lake cruises (€20–40) are worthwhile splurges.

- **Best for:** Couples seeking romance on the lakeshore, families who want easy city strolling, and solo travelers enjoying museums and markets.

11.2 Turin & the Italian Alps

Why Go:
Crossing into Italy for a day changes the rhythm entirely. Turin is sophisticated yet laid-back, a city where grand baroque squares meet artisan gelaterias and where the Alps provide a dramatic backdrop.

Highlights:

- **Piazza Castello & Via Roma:** Elegant squares framed by arcades, perfect for people-watching and espresso breaks.

- **The Egyptian Museum:** One of the most important collections outside Cairo, with fascinating mummies and artifacts.

- **Mole Antonelliana:** The symbol of Turin, housing the National Cinema Museum and offering panoramic views.

- **Markets:** Porta Palazzo is one of Europe's largest open-air markets, brimming with produce, cheese, and cured meats.

Cultural Touch:

Turin is the birthplace of slow food culture and home to iconic chocolate traditions. A must-try is **bicerin**, a layered drink of espresso, chocolate, and cream that has warmed locals since the 18th century.

Traveler Tips:

- **Transport:** From French Alpine towns like Modane or Chambéry, Turin is 2–3 hours by train (from €25). Driving through the Mont Blanc Tunnel adds toll costs (€60+ round trip).

- **Budget:** A day in Turin can be budget-friendly with pizza al taglio for €5, but a gourmet dinner in a trattoria may run €30–50 per person.

- **Best for:** Food lovers, art and film enthusiasts, and anyone curious about Italy's mix of refinement and warmth.

11.3 Lyon & the Rhône Valley

Why Go:
 Lyon, France's culinary capital, is an essential excursion for anyone interested in food, history, or the vibrant mix of Roman and Renaissance heritage. Beyond the city, the Rhône Valley offers rolling vineyards and charming riverside towns.

Highlights in Lyon:

- **Old Town (Vieux Lyon):** Narrow Renaissance lanes packed with bouchons (traditional restaurants) and secret passageways called traboules.

- **Basilica of Notre-Dame de Fourvière:** Climb the hill or ride the funicular for sweeping views over the city.

- **Les Halles de Lyon Paul Bocuse:** A covered market dedicated to the region's finest produce and artisanal specialties.

- **Roman Theaters:** Well-preserved amphitheaters host summer concerts and operas.

Highlights in the Rhône Valley:

- **Vineyards:** Côte-Rôtie, Hermitage, and Condrieu appellations are within easy reach for wine tastings.

- **Riverside Villages:** Tain-l'Hermitage and Vienne are perfect for strolls along the Rhône.

Traveler Tips:

- **Transport:** Trains from Annecy to Lyon take about 2 hours (€20–35). Car rentals offer flexibility for vineyard stops.

- **Budget:** Museum entry averages €8–12, bouchon menus range from €20–35, while wine tastings in the Rhône start around €15.

- **Best for:** Food lovers, history buffs, and families looking for a lively yet manageable city outing.

11.4 Provence & the Southern Alps

Why Go:
If Alpine air leaves you craving lavender fields and sunlit villages, Provence provides a contrasting landscape filled with sensory delights. The Southern Alps meanwhile bridge rugged mountain terrain with Provençal charm, offering quieter alternatives to busier Alpine resorts.

Highlights:

- **Lavender Routes:** In June and July, the Plateau de Valensole and Sault bloom with purple fields that perfume the air.

- **Hilltop Villages:** Gordes and Roussillon captivate with stone houses and ochre cliffs.

- **Verdon Gorge:** Known as Europe's Grand Canyon, perfect for kayaking, hiking, or scenic drives.

- **Southern Alpine Villages:** Places like Barcelonnette blend French and Mexican influences, a unique legacy from emigrant families.

Cultural Touch:
Provence is as much about rhythm as scenery. Days are marked by morning markets overflowing with olives, cheeses, and herbs, followed by leisurely lunches and evenings of pétanque in village squares.

Traveler Tips:

- **Transport:** By car, Provence is 3–4 hours from Annecy, making it best for an overnight excursion. Train connections are also possible via Valence or Avignon.

- **Budget:** Lavender tours are often free if self-guided; kayak rentals in Verdon Gorge cost €20–35; market lunches can be as little as €10–15.

- **Best for:** Couples seeking romance, photographers, and anyone wanting to balance Alpine peaks with Provençal sunshine.

11.5 Cross-Border Ski & Hike Adventures

Why Go:
One of the Alps' greatest advantages is the ease of crossing borders. Skiers and hikers can hop between France, Switzerland, and Italy in a single outing, experiencing cultural variety without long travel times.

Highlights:

- **The Mont Blanc Massif:** From Chamonix, take the Aiguille du Midi cable car (€70 return) and cross into Courmayeur, Italy. Skiers can enjoy different runs on each side in winter, while summer brings high-altitude hikes with unmatched views.

- **The Portes du Soleil:** A ski domain linking French resorts like Morzine and Avoriaz with Swiss villages such as Champéry. Lift passes cover the whole circuit (€65 per day).

- **Summer Trails:** Cross-border hikes like the Tour du Mont Blanc weave through France, Italy, and Switzerland, with options for single-day sections or multi-day treks.

Cultural Touch:

Crossing borders is not only about landscapes but also flavors. Lunch in Switzerland might mean rösti and local cheese, while dinner back in France brings tartiflette or fondue.

Traveler Tips:

- **Transport:** Regional buses and ski shuttles make access straightforward, but having a car offers maximum flexibility.

- **Budget:** Lift passes vary by resort but expect €60–70 per day. Hut stays during summer treks cost €40–70 including meals.

- **Best for:** Adventurous travelers, families with older children, and anyone curious about blending cultures within a single excursion.

11.6 Suggested Mini Itineraries for Day Trips

To tie these excursions together, here are a few sample journeys:

A Day of Lakes and Diplomacy (Annecy – Geneva – Lake Cruise):
Morning train to Geneva, tour the UN, lunch in the Old Town, and an afternoon boat cruise before returning to the Alps. Perfect for travelers with limited time but a desire for international flavor.

Alpine-to-Italian Flavor (Chamonix – Courmayeur – Turin):
Start with a morning cable car across Mont Blanc into Courmayeur for espresso and mountain views, then continue to Turin for an evening of piazza dining before returning.

Gastronomy and Vineyards (Annecy – Lyon – Rhône Valley):
Spend the morning exploring Vieux Lyon, enjoy lunch in a bouchon, then head south for an afternoon tasting in Tain-l'Hermitage before a scenic return train.

Chapter 12: Responsible & Sustainable Travel in the Alps

The Alps inspire travelers with their peaks, meadows, lakes, and villages, but they are also among the most fragile ecosystems in Europe. Rising temperatures, shrinking glaciers, and increasing tourist flows put stress on both the environment and the communities who live here year-round. Choosing to travel responsibly is not about giving up comfort or adventure; it is about making choices that help preserve the landscapes and traditions you have come to admire. From selecting where to sleep to how you move around, what you eat, and whom you support, every decision can contribute to a healthier future for the Alps.

12.1 Eco-Friendly Accommodation & Transport

Staying Green in the Alps

Accommodation makes up a significant portion of your travel footprint. Fortunately, the Alps offer a wide range of eco-conscious stays that balance comfort with responsibility.

- **Eco-Lodges and Green Hotels:** Many chalets and boutique hotels now operate with renewable energy, water recycling, and strict waste management. Labels like the EU Ecolabel or Green Key guarantee certain standards.

- **Mountain Huts:** Staying in a *refuge* or alpine hut is both traditional and eco-friendly. Many huts rely on solar panels and local food supplies. Hiking to your hut rather than driving adds to the sustainability.

- **Farm Stays:** Rural guesthouses allow travelers to connect with local families, enjoy seasonal produce, and directly support agricultural traditions.

Prices for eco-lodges and mountain huts vary: huts often charge €40–70 per night including meals, while mid-range eco-hotels range €90–150.

Greener Ways to Travel

Transport is one of the biggest contributors to carbon emissions in Alpine tourism. The good news is that the region's rail network is efficient, scenic, and increasingly electrified.

- **Trains:** Direct lines connect Paris, Geneva, Turin, Munich, and Zurich with Alpine hubs like Annecy, Chamonix, Innsbruck, and Zermatt. Advance bookings often bring fares down to €30–60.

- **Buses and Shared Transfers:** From airports and city centers, shared shuttle services are far more eco-friendly than private cars.

- **Cycling and E-Bikes:** Many resorts now have bike-share programs, allowing visitors to replace short car trips with pedal power.

- **Walking-Friendly Villages:** Places like Zermatt and Wengen restrict cars entirely, offering clean air and a slower pace.

Traveler Tip: When possible, choose direct train routes over short-haul flights. A single train ride can reduce your emissions by up to 80 percent compared to flying.

12.2 Reducing Your Environmental Impact

Mindful Adventures

Alpine trails and ski slopes attract millions, but each visitor has an impact. Adopting low-impact practices ensures that these landscapes remain pristine.

- **Leave No Trace:** Carry back all waste, including biodegradable items like orange peels.

- **Stick to Paths:** Straying from trails can damage alpine plants that take years to recover.

- **Reusable Gear:** Bring refillable water bottles, reusable utensils, and cloth bags to minimize single-use plastics.

- **Water and Energy Use:** Alpine villages sometimes face water shortages in summer. Take short showers, avoid unnecessary laundry, and switch off lights and heating when not in use.

Dining Responsibly

The food you eat also leaves an imprint. Choosing seasonal, local ingredients helps reduce transportation emissions and supports farmers. Opt for mountain cheeses, cured meats, and alpine vegetables rather than imported produce. Many restaurants now highlight regional specialties with "zero-kilometer" labels, meaning ingredients come from within the valley.

Winter Tourism Choices

Snowmaking has become common as winters grow shorter, but it consumes large amounts of water and energy. Seek out ski resorts that manage resources responsibly, or balance skiing with other activities like snowshoeing, which require less infrastructure.

12.3 Supporting Local Communities

Shopping and Souvenirs

Supporting local economies makes your trip more meaningful. Choose hand-carved wooden ornaments, locally woven textiles, or artisanal cheeses over mass-produced souvenirs. Markets and village shops are excellent places to find such items.

Dining and Accommodation

Whenever possible, eat in family-owned restaurants and stay in independent hotels or guesthouses. Not only does this circulate money within the community, it also gives you a more authentic experience of Alpine hospitality.

Participating in Local Life

Engaging with cultural traditions shows respect for the people who keep these customs alive.

Traveler Tip: Ask locals where they shop, eat, and relax. Often, the best recommendations are those not featured in guidebooks, and your spending will directly benefit residents.

12.4 Alpine Wildlife & Conservation Projects

The Fragility of Alpine Wildlife

The Alps are home to marmots, ibex, chamois, golden eagles, and countless smaller species. However, habitat loss and climate change put pressure on biodiversity. Encountering wildlife is a highlight for many travelers, but it should always be done with care.

- **Observation, Not Interaction:** Keep safe distances and avoid feeding animals, which disrupts natural behavior.

- **Seasonal Awareness:** Some trails close during breeding or nesting seasons to protect species. Respect closures.

Conservation in Action

Several organizations and parks are actively working to preserve Alpine ecosystems:

- **Vanoise National Park (France):** Home to ibex conservation programs.

- **Swiss National Park:** The oldest national park in the Alps, with strict "no disturbance" policies.

- **Alparc (Alpine Network of Protected Areas):** A collaborative initiative uniting parks across multiple countries.

Visitors can contribute by joining volunteer programs, such as trail maintenance days or citizen science projects like bird counts.

Traveler Tip: Many parks request a small entrance fee (€5–10). Consider it a donation to protect landscapes for future visitors.

12.5 The Future of Sustainable Alpine Tourism

The Alps are at the frontlines of climate change. Glaciers are retreating, snowlines are rising, and traditional ways of life are adapting. Tourism must evolve to ensure that future generations can enjoy these landscapes.

Shifting Seasons

The reliance on winter skiing is changing as snow becomes less predictable. Resorts are diversifying with year-round offers like hiking, cycling, cultural events, and wellness tourism. Travelers who embrace multi-season activities help reduce pressure on winter resources.

Green Innovation

Technologies are reshaping Alpine tourism:

- Solar-powered lifts and huts.

- Electric shuttle fleets connecting ski villages.

- Smart ticketing systems encouraging car-free travel.

Education and Awareness

Future Alpine tourism will depend on traveler choices. As awareness grows, visitors are increasingly willing to pay a small premium for sustainable options. Transparent certification schemes will help separate genuine eco-efforts from "greenwashing."

Traveler Tip: When choosing tour operators or accommodations, look for transparency in their sustainability policies rather than vague claims. Ask where their energy comes from, how they handle waste, and how they support local employment.

Traveling responsibly in the Alps is not a limitation but an invitation to connect more deeply with the region. By choosing eco-friendly accommodations, reducing waste, supporting local craftspeople, respecting wildlife, and thinking about the future of tourism, you contribute to the preservation of Europe's most iconic mountain range. Sustainable travel also enriches your own experience: meals taste better when ingredients come from a nearby farm, hikes feel more rewarding when you know you are helping protect fragile ecosystems, and interactions with locals are warmer when they know you value their traditions.

Chapter 13: Safety, Health & Accessibility

The French Alps welcome millions of visitors each year, drawn by their beauty and the range of activities on offer. Yet behind the postcard-perfect peaks lie realities that every traveler must respect. High altitudes, rapidly shifting weather, and mountain terrain demand preparation. Beyond physical safety, visitors must also consider health care access, the needs of children or elderly family members, and the inclusivity of travel for those with disabilities. With foresight and the right tools, the Alps can be an accessible, safe, and enriching destination for everyone.

13.1 Staying Safe in Alpine Terrain

Understanding Mountain Conditions

The Alps' beauty can be deceptive. Weather can shift from sunshine to storm in minutes, and even short walks can become dangerous if you are unprepared. Always check forecasts before leaving your accommodation, especially if you plan to hike, ski, or drive mountain passes. Local tourism offices and ski stations provide daily updates on avalanche risks, trail conditions, and open routes.

Hiking & Trekking Safety

- **Stay on Marked Paths:** Alpine vegetation is fragile, and off-path wandering increases risks of falls.

- **Carry Essentials:** Even for short walks, pack water, snacks, a basic first aid kit, and a charged phone.

- **Time Your Routes:** Darkness falls quickly in valleys; plan to return well before sunset.

Skiing & Snowboarding Safety

Winter sports bring their own set of risks.

- **Helmets:** Strongly recommended for all ages and mandatory for children in many ski schools.

- **Know Your Level:** Do not attempt slopes above your ability; green and blue pistes are best for beginners, while red and black slopes are for advanced skiers.

- **Avalanche Awareness:** Off-piste skiing should only be attempted with a guide and proper safety equipment.

General Mountain Hazards

- **Altitude Sickness:** Symptoms like dizziness, nausea, or shortness of breath can occur above 2,500 meters. Acclimatize gradually and drink plenty of water.

- **Sun Protection:** UV rays are stronger at altitude, even in winter. Use sunscreen and wear sunglasses with UV protection.

- **Driving Risks:** Mountain roads may be narrow and winding. Winter requires snow tires or chains.

Traveler Tip: Local guides, available for €100–200 per day, not only enhance your experience but also ensure safer exploration.

13.2 Healthcare, Pharmacies & Emergency Numbers

Medical Facilities

France has excellent healthcare, and Alpine regions are no exception. Most medium-sized towns, such as Grenoble, Annecy, or Chamonix, have hospitals with emergency departments. Smaller ski villages often rely on medical centers staffed by general practitioners and physiotherapists trained in treating sports injuries.

- **Cost:** A doctor's consultation in France typically costs €25–50. Emergency care is higher, but European Health Insurance Card (EHIC) holders and some international insurance plans reduce costs.

- **Specialist Care:** Sports injury clinics are common in ski resorts, treating sprains, fractures, and dislocations.

Pharmacies

Pharmacies are easy to identify by their green neon cross signs. They are well-stocked with common medicines, first-aid supplies, and remedies for altitude sickness or stomach upsets. In rural areas, note opening hours, as many close midday and on Sundays. Emergency pharmacies (*pharmacie de garde*) are posted on local doors or available by calling emergency numbers.

Emergency Services

- **General Emergency (Police, Fire, Ambulance):** 112

- **Mountain Rescue (PGHM):** 17 or direct via 112

- **Ambulance (SAMU):** 15

Operators often speak English in tourist areas, but learning a few French phrases helps.

Traveler Tip: If calling for help in the mountains, be prepared to provide your GPS coordinates or a clear landmark description. Apps like

Géolocalisation 112 can transmit your location to rescuers.

13.3 Accessibility for Travelers with Disabilities

The French Alps are increasingly committed to inclusive tourism. While rugged terrain poses challenges, many resorts, towns, and cultural sites have adapted facilities.

Adaptive Skiing & Outdoor Sports

Specialized equipment and instructors make skiing possible for visitors with limited mobility or visual impairments. Resorts like Les Gets and La Plagne are leaders in adaptive skiing, offering sit-skis, guiding services, and trained staff. Prices for adaptive lessons are similar to regular ski schools, around €50–80 per hour.

Accessible Towns and Transport

- **Annecy & Grenoble:** Both cities have accessible public transport, wheelchair-friendly lakeside promenades, and adapted museums.

- **Cable Cars:** Many gondolas, such as the Aiguille du Midi in Chamonix, are wheelchair accessible. Staff assist with boarding.

- **Trains:** French TGVs and regional TER trains provide reserved wheelchair spaces, ramps, and staff support when booked in advance.

Accommodation

Many hotels and chalets comply with France's disability access regulations, offering step-free entrances, adapted bathrooms, and elevators. Booking platforms often filter by accessibility features.

Traveler Tip: Contact hotels or resorts directly before booking to confirm facilities match your needs. Standards vary widely, especially in older buildings.

13.4 Traveling with Kids & Elderly Family Members

Family-Friendly Adventures

The Alps are not just for thrill-seekers. Families with children will find dedicated ski schools, play areas, and gentle slopes.

- **Ski Kindergartens:** For children as young as 3, these offer half-day programs starting from €30–50.

- **Indoor Activities:** Aquatic centers, climbing gyms, and cultural workshops keep kids entertained during bad weather.

Safety Tips for Kids

- Bright clothing helps children stay visible on slopes or trails.

- Wristbands with parents' contact details are recommended for crowded ski resorts.

- Helmets are essential for skiing, cycling, or climbing.

Elderly Travelers

Older visitors often enjoy the Alps through wellness retreats, scenic rail rides, and gentle walks.

- **Wellness & Spas:** Thermal towns like Aix-les-Bains offer therapeutic treatments for joints and circulation.

- **Cable Cars & Scenic Routes:** These provide alpine views without strenuous hiking.

- **Mobility Considerations:** Some towns have steep cobbled streets, so sturdy walking shoes and canes are useful.

Traveler Tip: Consider staying in resorts with flat terrain (e.g., Morzine or Les Saisies) if traveling with elderly family members.

13.5 Insurance & Safety Gear Essentials

Travel Insurance

Comprehensive travel insurance is vital. Policies should cover:

- Emergency medical care and evacuation.

- Winter sports accidents.

- Lost luggage or equipment.

- Trip cancellations due to weather or illness.

Expect policies to cost €40–80 per week, depending on coverage and age. Always check that high-altitude activities like off-piste skiing or paragliding are included.

Safety Gear Essentials

Packing the right gear reduces risks:

- **For Hikers:** Waterproof boots, layered clothing, maps, trekking poles, headlamp.

- **For Skiers:** Helmet, goggles, avalanche beacon, probe, and shovel if off-piste.

- **For Drivers:** Snow chains, reflective vest, and warning triangle (required by French law).

Rental vs. Purchase

Gear rental is widely available in resorts, from skis to avalanche packs. Renting costs around €25–40 per day, while purchasing is only worthwhile for frequent travelers.

Traveler Tip: Consider renting safety gear locally rather than carrying it across borders. This reduces baggage stress and ensures your equipment meets current standards.

Safety, health, and accessibility form the backbone of a successful Alpine trip. Preparing for changing mountain conditions, knowing where to find healthcare, traveling inclusively, and carrying the right insurance all transform potential risks into manageable details. The Alps are not just for the young, fit, or fearless—they are for families, older travelers, and people with varied abilities who wish to embrace nature, culture, and wellness.

By balancing adventure with awareness, you ensure not only your own safety but also the wellbeing of those who travel alongside you. The French Alps, with their peaks and valleys, are best experienced with respect—for the terrain, for your health, and for the communities that host you.

Chapter 14: Capturing the Alps: Photography & Iconic Views

The French Alps are not just a playground for skiers, hikers, and adventurers—they are also a living canvas for photographers. From soft dawn light on snow-capped peaks to the fiery hues of sunsets reflecting on alpine lakes, the region offers endless opportunities to capture the kind of images that both professionals and casual travelers dream of. Each season, village, and viewpoint holds its own magic, making the Alps one of Europe's most photographed destinations.

In this chapter, we explore the best places and times to photograph, practical etiquette for drone and landscape photography, seasonal approaches to storytelling through images, and the most social media-friendly locations that resonate with today's travelers.

14.1 Best Sunrise & Sunset Spots

The Alps are defined by dramatic light. The combination of high peaks, reflective snow, and deep valleys creates a natural stage where light shifts rapidly throughout the day. Sunrise and sunset are especially magical, transforming the mountains into shades of gold, pink, and violet.

Chamonix & Mont Blanc at Dawn
Perhaps nowhere is more iconic than Chamonix, with Mont Blanc towering above. Early morning light often paints the summit in pink before cascading down the ridges. The Aiguille du Midi cable car (around €70 return) provides a breathtaking perspective for photographers, especially in winter when the snow is at its purest.

Annecy Lake at Sunset
The medieval town of Annecy is best captured from the Pont des Amours bridge as the sun dips behind the surrounding mountains. The lake reflects soft pastel skies, while the town's canals glow with golden light. Evening boat rentals (around €20–€30 per hour) allow for unique compositions from the water.

Lac Blanc in the Chamonix Valley

 A favorite among hikers and photographers, Lac Blanc reflects Mont Blanc like a natural mirror. Reaching it requires a moderate hike (2–3 hours), but those who stay overnight in the Lac Blanc refuge can capture both sunrise and sunset with almost no crowds.

Val d'Isère & Tignes

 High-altitude resorts like Val d'Isère offer elevated platforms for photographing sunsets across the peaks. The Col de l'Iseran, accessible by car in summer, is particularly striking in golden hour light.

Traveler Tip:

For winter photography, carry extra batteries as cold temperatures drain them quickly. A hand warmer in your camera bag can extend battery life significantly.

14.2 Alpine Lakes, Peaks & Villages to Photograph

Beyond sunrises and sunsets, the Alps are filled with year-round photographic gems: mirror-like lakes, dramatic peaks, and charming villages that seem frozen in time.

Mirror Lakes

- *Lac d'Annecy*: Known as Europe's cleanest lake, its turquoise waters look spectacular when paired with paddle boats, swans, or the surrounding medieval town.

- *Lac de Serre-Ponçon*: A massive alpine reservoir offering bold blue water framed by rugged cliffs. Great for drone shots (where permitted).

- *Lac Vert*: Nestled in Passy, this emerald-green lake is small but highly photogenic with Mont Blanc looming in the background.

Iconic Peaks

- *Mont Blanc*: The roof of Western Europe is visible from numerous vantage points, but Les Houches and the Aiguille du Midi provide some of the best framing.

- *Aiguilles d'Arves*: These three jagged peaks near Valloire create a dramatic silhouette against the sky, best captured in the late afternoon.

- *Dent du Géant*: Near Chamonix, this "Giant's Tooth" peak makes for striking images, especially with climbers ascending its ridges.

Storybook Villages

- *Megève*: Its wooden chalets, horse-drawn carriages, and cobblestone streets look straight out of a fairy tale, particularly in winter snow.

- *Les Gets*: Known for its traditional farmhouses and ski-in, ski-out charm, it's a great setting for lifestyle photography.

- *Yvoire*: On the shores of Lake Geneva, this medieval village blooms with flowers in summer and provides colorful street scenes.

Traveler Tip:
Villages are best photographed in the morning when streets are less crowded. In winter, snow adds brightness, while in summer, flower boxes on chalets provide pops of color.

14.3 Drone & Travel Photography Etiquette

The Alps attract drone photographers keen to capture sweeping aerial views of valleys, glaciers, and ski resorts. However, regulations and etiquette are critical.

Drone Regulations

- France requires drones over 800 g to be registered.

- Flying near airports, heliports, or crowded ski resorts is prohibited.

- National parks and protected natural areas often restrict drone use.

Always check local rules before flying. Apps like *Geoportail* and *Drone Assist* show permitted zones. Fines for illegal flights can reach €15,000.

Etiquette in Villages & Trails

- Avoid flying over private property without permission.

- Respect hikers' and skiers' peace by limiting noise.

- Do not disturb wildlife—especially ibex, marmots, and birds of prey that inhabit alpine zones.

General Photography Etiquette

- In villages, ask before photographing locals in traditional attire, especially during festivals.

- Use discretion in religious sites, such as mountain chapels.

- Avoid flash when photographing artwork or in dim interiors.

Traveler Tip:
If drones are restricted, use wide-angle lenses from elevated viewpoints for a similar sweeping effect.

14.4 Seasonal Photo Themes (Winter vs. Summer)

Each season in the Alps transforms the landscape into a completely different photographic subject. Knowing how to approach each season enhances your portfolio.

Winter (December–March)
 Snow blankets villages and peaks, offering high-contrast images. Look for:

- Skiers in motion with mountains in the background.

- Frozen lakes with snow-dusted pines.

- Christmas markets glowing with fairy lights. Bluebird days after snowstorms are especially striking.

Spring (April–June)

Melting snow gives way to wildflowers and waterfalls. Themes include:

- Rolling meadows filled with alpine blossoms.

- Villages framed by both snow peaks and budding trees.

- Rushing rivers from glacier melt.

Summer (July–September)

The high mountains become accessible, making hiking photography prime. Capture:

- Crystal-clear lakes like Lac Blanc or Lac de Roselend.

- Pastoral scenes of cows grazing with cowbells.

- Outdoor festivals and lively town squares.

Autumn (October–November)
Golden larch forests and quiet valleys create painterly images. Themes:

- Vibrant orange foliage against snowy ridges.

- Empty hiking trails bathed in warm afternoon light.

- Vineyard harvests in the Rhône Valley and Savoie.

Traveler Tip:
Carry a polarizing filter for summer and autumn shots—it deepens blue skies, reduces glare on lakes, and makes colors pop.

14.5 Social Media-Friendly Locations

With Instagram and TikTok influencing travel choices more than ever, certain locations in the French Alps have gained a reputation as photogenic hotspots.

Annecy's Old Town
The pastel buildings, flower-bedecked canals, and the Palais de l'Isle fortress are endlessly shareable. Early morning offers soft light without crowds.

Chamonix's Montenvers Railway
The red cogwheel train against a snowy backdrop feels like stepping into a postcard. It leads to the Mer de Glace glacier, where dramatic shots abound.

Aiguille du Midi Skywalk
The glass platform at 3,842 meters is one of the most adrenaline-inducing photo spots in Europe. Selfies here often go viral.

Val Thorens Igloo Village

An ice hotel with sculpted walls and glowing interiors makes for unusual winter photography. Staying overnight costs around €120 per person.

Lavender & Alps Combo in Provence

In July, travelers can combine lavender fields near Valensole with the distant snow-topped Alps for unique contrasts that dominate social feeds.

Traveler Tip:

If aiming for viral shots, look for angles that haven't been overdone. Instead of repeating the same selfie, capture locals at work, unexpected weather moods, or details like frost on a chalet window.

Mini Photography Itineraries

To help photographers plan their time, here are sample itineraries based on trip length and focus:

One-Day Photography Tour (Chamonix Valley)

- Sunrise at Lac Blanc (hike or refuge overnight).

- Mid-morning shots from Aiguille du Midi cable car.

- Afternoon lifestyle photography in Chamonix town.

- Sunset at the Mer de Glace from Montenvers Railway.

Three-Day Photographer's Journey (Annecy & Surroundings)

- Day 1: Sunrise on Lake Annecy, capture canals and medieval streets.

- Day 2: Visit Lac Vert and alpine meadows near Passy.

- Day 3: Explore Yvoire on Lake Geneva for historic village shots.

Five-Day Mixed Season Portfolio

- Day 1: Winter village scenes in Megève.

- Day 2: Sunrise at Val d'Isère peaks.

- Day 3: Summer hiking shots at Lac de Roselend.

- Day 4: Autumn foliage in the Tarentaise Valley.

- Day 5: Cultural street scenes at a local farmers' market.

Capturing the French Alps is about more than just pointing a camera at mountains. It is about storytelling: the interplay of light and shadow, the rhythm of seasons, and the human presence that makes the Alps both a natural wonder and a cultural landscape. Whether you are shooting with a professional DSLR, a drone, or simply your smartphone, the key is to slow down, observe, and let the mountains reveal their many moods.

Photography in the Alps is an invitation not just to witness beauty but to frame it in a way that shares your personal journey. Each sunrise, each village corner, and each snow-dusted ridge becomes part of a narrative you carry home, long after the moment has passed.

Chapter 15: Shopping, Souvenirs & Local Markets

The French Alps are not only a destination for adventurers and culture seekers but also a paradise for those who love browsing unique shops, lively markets, and artisan workshops. Shopping here is not about malls or mass production. Instead, it is an invitation to take home a piece of alpine tradition, whether in the form of handmade crafts, local foods, or durable outdoor gear designed for mountain life.

This chapter explores the best ways to shop in the region: where to find authentic goods, what foods to pack in your bag, and how to support local communities responsibly. From woodcarvers in remote villages to chocolatiers in bustling towns, every purchase tells a story of heritage, skill, and connection to the landscape.

15.1 Artisan Crafts & Handmade Goods

The French Alps have a long history of craftsmanship, rooted in necessity but elevated into artistry. Remote mountain living encouraged locals to create practical tools, furniture, and clothing, but over centuries these evolved into decorative objects admired by visitors.

Woodcarving & Sculptures
Villages like Morzine, Megève, and Les Gets are renowned for wooden crafts. You'll find everything from carved cowbells and alpine figurines to ornate furniture. Prices range from small keychains (€5–€10) to elaborate handmade chairs (€150–€400).

Textiles & Wool Products
The harsh winters made wool an essential part of alpine life. Local artisans still spin and weave traditional blankets, scarves, and socks, often using wool from sheep grazing nearby. Authentic handmade wool items can cost around €40–€70, while machine-assisted products are cheaper.

Ceramics & Pottery

In towns such as Thonon-les-Bains or Annecy, you'll come across pottery studios producing rustic bowls, mugs, and plates decorated with alpine motifs. These make excellent souvenirs that are functional and durable. Expect to pay €15–€30 for mugs or €40–€80 for serving bowls.

Jewelry & Small Crafts

Many jewelers incorporate natural elements such as mountain flowers, dried edelweiss, or even tiny quartz crystals found in alpine streams. Small pendants start around €20, while silver or gold pieces with detailed craftsmanship can exceed €200.

Traveler Tip: If buying wooden or ceramic souvenirs, consider the weight and fragility when traveling. Wrap items in clothing inside your luggage or ship them home from a local post office.

15.2 Local Foods, Cheeses & Chocolates to Take Home

Food is one of the most rewarding souvenirs from the French Alps, and it offers a way to relive the experience long after the trip is over. The region is particularly proud of its cheeses, chocolates, cured meats, and jams—all products tied deeply to alpine tradition.

Cheeses of the Alps

- *Reblochon*: Creamy and aromatic, this is the heart of tartiflette. A wheel costs around €8–€12 and can usually be vacuum-sealed for travel.

- *Beaufort*: Known as the "Prince of Gruyères," it is firmer, nutty, and excellent for melting. Prices average €20–€25 per kilo.

- *Tomme de Savoie*: Rustic, earthy, and often sold in wedges. Expect €10–€15 for a medium-sized piece.

Most cheese shops will vacuum-pack purchases, making them safe for flights if customs regulations allow.

Chocolates & Sweets

Artisan chocolatiers in Grenoble, Annecy, and Chambéry produce pralines, truffles, and bars infused with mountain flavors such as génépi liqueur or blueberries. Boxes typically cost between €10–€30, depending on size and craftsmanship.

Cured Meats & Sausages

Savoyard *saucisson sec* (dry sausage) and mountain hams are popular souvenirs, with prices ranging from €6–€15 per sausage. These are often sold at outdoor markets and packaged for easy transport.

Honey & Jams

Alpine meadows produce aromatic honeys from wildflowers, lavender, or chestnut trees. A jar costs around €7–€12. Blueberry and raspberry jams are also common, often sold in decorative jars suitable for gifts.

Spirits & Liqueurs

- *Génépi*: A herbal liqueur made from a rare alpine plant. Small bottles start at €15.

- *Chartreuse*: Distilled by Carthusian monks near Grenoble, this comes in green and yellow varieties with distinct herbal notes. A bottle costs around €35–€50.

Traveler Tip: Always check your home country's customs rules regarding food imports. Many allow hard cheeses and sealed products but restrict fresh dairy or meats.

15.3 Outdoor Gear & Alpine Fashion

Shopping in the Alps also means preparing for the elements. The region is a hub for high-quality outdoor gear, blending fashion with practicality.

Performance Gear
Chamonix and Grenoble are hotspots for technical equipment. Brands like Millet, Salomon, and Rossignol were born in the Alps and remain leaders in skis, boots, jackets, and backpacks. Jackets start around €150, while professional-grade skis range from €400–€800.

Alpine Fashion

Beyond sports gear, alpine fashion has evolved into a blend of rustic charm and chic style. Think wool sweaters, fur-lined boots, and stylish après-ski outfits. In resort towns like Courchevel or Megève, luxury boutiques sell designer winter clothing. Expect to pay €200–€600 for branded coats and accessories.

Sustainable Gear

With growing interest in eco-conscious shopping, many shops now stock recycled-material jackets, bamboo-fiber shirts, and biodegradable ski wax. These can be more expensive but support sustainable practices.

Traveler Tip: Buying gear in the Alps ensures authenticity and often provides better quality than generic brands elsewhere. Look for seasonal sales in spring and autumn for discounts up to 50 percent.

15.4 Traditional Markets Worth Visiting

One of the best shopping experiences in the Alps is wandering through traditional markets. These are as much about atmosphere as they are about goods, offering a blend of food, crafts, and social life.

Annecy Market
Held on Tuesdays, Fridays, and Sundays, this market spills through the old town. Stalls sell cheeses, fresh bread, sausages, flowers, and crafts. It's especially photogenic along the canals.

Chambéry Market
This historic market takes place on Saturdays and is known for regional products like Beaufort cheese, wines, and handmade crafts. It's lively and attracts both locals and visitors.

Grenoble's Saint-Claire Market
One of the largest, with over 100 stalls offering everything from mountain honey to textiles. Saturday mornings are the busiest.

Megève's Seasonal Markets
During winter and summer, Megève hosts special artisan markets featuring woodcrafts, wool goods, and gourmet products.

Traveler Tip: Bring cash, as many smaller stalls may not accept cards. Arrive early for the best selection and fewer crowds. Sampling before buying is encouraged, especially for cheeses and sausages.

15.5 What Not to Buy: Ethical Shopping Tips

Responsible shopping means making informed choices. While the Alps offer many authentic products, not everything sold is sustainable or respectful of traditions.

Avoid Mass-Produced Souvenirs
Plastic cowbells, cheaply made "alpine hats," or souvenirs stamped with "Made in China" do little to support local communities.

Be Careful with Wildlife Products
Do not buy items made from protected species such as eagle feathers, ibex horns, or real edelweiss flowers. Many of these are illegal and harmful to ecosystems.

Question "Traditional" Labels
Some shops market mass-produced goods as "artisan." To ensure authenticity, buy directly from workshops or certified cooperatives.

Support Local, Not Just Luxury
High-end boutiques in resorts may sell international brands rather than regional products. For a meaningful souvenir, seek out smaller producers.

Traveler Tip: Ask vendors about the origin of their goods. Most artisans are proud to share their story, and this ensures your purchase contributes to the local economy.

Suggested Mini Itineraries for Shoppers

One-Day Shopping Tour in Annecy

- Morning: Explore the old town market, sampling cheeses and chocolates.

- Afternoon: Visit artisan pottery workshops near the canals.

- Evening: Browse small boutiques for wool scarves and handmade jewelry.

Three-Day Alpine Souvenir Adventure

- Day 1: Grenoble market for honey, jams, and Chartreuse liqueur.

- Day 2: Chamonix gear shops for authentic outdoor equipment.

- Day 3: Megève artisan fair for wood carvings and wool goods.

Luxury Meets Local (Weekend in Megève)

- Morning: Designer alpine fashion boutiques.

- Afternoon: Visit a cooperative cheese dairy for Reblochon and Beaufort.

- Evening: Purchase handmade ceramics as gifts.

Shopping in the French Alps is more than acquiring things—it is about discovering stories. A carved wooden figurine represents a craftsman's heritage, a wedge of Beaufort connects you to alpine pastures, and a handmade wool scarf carries the warmth of the mountains into your daily life.

Bonus 1: Essential French Phrases & Cultural Etiquette

Why Language and Etiquette Matter in the French Alps

Picture yourself stepping into a rustic boulangerie in Annecy, the smell of fresh baguettes wafting through the air. You point to a croissant and say in English, "One, please." The baker pauses politely but without much warmth. Then you recall the phrase you practiced earlier: *"Bonjour, un croissant, s'il vous plaît."* The baker's face softens, and the exchange feels different — more human, more personal. This small effort in French transforms a transaction into a connection. That is the essence of traveling in the Alps: landscapes impress you, but people define your experience.

The French Alps receive millions of international visitors each year, and English is widely understood in resorts and hotels. Still, depending entirely on it can create a distance. Politeness, patience, and a willingness to try even a few words in French show respect for the culture.

181

The Ritual of Greetings

Nowhere is etiquette more important than in greetings. In France, a greeting is not optional; it is the foundation of social exchange. Whether entering a bakery, ski rental shop, or village grocery store, start with a clear *"Bonjour"* in the morning or *"Bonsoir"* in the evening. Skip this step, and you may notice a subtle coolness in the response. Add a polite *"merci"* when leaving, and you leave a positive impression.

In Alpine towns, greetings stretch beyond shops. On hiking trails, strangers acknowledge one another with a nod or a cheerful *"bonjour."* To say nothing feels awkward in this context. These moments are small but powerful, weaving you into the rhythm of daily Alpine life.

Dining Etiquette in Mountain Restaurants

Meals in the French Alps are a cultural ritual as much as a way to refuel after a long ski run. Imagine sitting at a wooden table in Chamonix, a pot of bubbling fondue placed in front of you. The etiquette here is not about strict rules but about respect for shared traditions. When ordering, soften requests with *"Je voudrais..."* rather than blunt statements. It signals courtesy, even if the waiter speaks to you in English afterward.

Dishes like fondue or raclette are communal by nature, and etiquette plays a role in how they are enjoyed. Avoid double-dipping and take turns, treating the meal as a shared experience rather than an individual plate. At the end, linger a little. Meals in the Alps are meant for conversation, not rushing. A final *"merci, c'était très bon"* shows appreciation for both the food and the service.

Markets and Everyday Encounters

Weekly markets are a highlight of Alpine life. Stalls brim with wheels of Beaufort cheese, cured sausages, jars of honey, and fresh herbs. These spaces are more than commercial; they are social gatherings. Vendors are proud of their products and enjoy explaining differences if you ask. Begin with *"Bonjour"* and perhaps *"Puis-je goûter?"* when requesting a sample. Bargaining is uncommon in France, so focus on friendliness rather than negotiation.

Cash is useful in small markets where vendors may not accept cards. After a purchase, a warm *"merci, bonne journée"* is a small but meaningful gesture. This exchange is not about efficiency; it is about connecting with people who carry on the traditions of Alpine farming and craftsmanship.

On the Slopes and Après-Ski

The ski slopes introduce their own form of etiquette. While instructors in Chamonix or Megève often teach in English, a few phrases like *"plus vite"* (faster) or *"plus lentement"* (slower) may still appear during lessons. Beyond language, etiquette is about respecting space. Queue calmly for lifts, yield to skiers downhill from you, and follow posted signs.

Après-ski is where etiquette shifts to sociability. Whether sipping hot chocolate in a family café or raising a glass of génépi in a lively bar, toasting with *"santé"* or *"à la vôtre"* includes you in the circle. These small rituals remind you that skiing is not only a sport but a cultural rhythm in the Alps.

Social Interactions and Daily Politeness

Beyond restaurants and slopes, etiquette guides ordinary encounters. A handshake is the standard greeting when introduced to someone new, though close friends may exchange "bises," the traditional cheek kisses. In rural areas, even strangers acknowledge each other on the street with a nod or greeting. Entering any shop or small business without saying *"bonjour"* can feel cold to locals, while a warm *"au revoir"* on your way out leaves a good impression.

Certain behaviors stand out as un-French. Speaking loudly on public transport is frowned upon. Eating while walking is uncommon; locals prefer to sit and savor. In photography, avoid taking close shots of strangers without asking. And above all, respect nature: Alpine communities take pride in protecting their environment, and leaving litter or damaging trails will not go unnoticed.

Essential Phrases

Greetings and Everyday Courtesies

- Bonjour – Hello / Good morning

- Bonsoir – Good evening

- Au revoir – Goodbye

- Bonne journée – Have a good day

- S'il vous plaît – Please

- Merci beaucoup – Thank you very much

- Excusez-moi – Excuse me

Shopping and Market Encounters

- Combien ça coûte ? – How much does it cost?

- Puis-je goûter ? – May I taste?

- C'est local ? – Is it local?

187

- Je voudrais… – I would like…

- Trois, s'il vous plaît – Three, please

Dining Out and Ordering Food

- Une table pour deux, s'il vous plaît – A table for two, please

- Je voudrais la raclette – I would like the raclette

- Qu'est-ce que vous conseillez ? – What do you recommend?

- Je suis végétarien(ne) – I am vegetarian

- Je suis allergique aux noix – I am allergic to nuts

- L'addition, s'il vous plaît – The bill, please

- Merci, c'était délicieux – Thank you, it was delicious

Hotels and Accommodation

- J'ai une réservation au nom de... – I have a reservation under the name...

- Avez-vous une chambre disponible ? – Do you have a room available?

- À quelle heure est le petit déjeuner ? – What time is breakfast?

- Le wifi est-il compris ? – Is the Wi-Fi included?

- Parlez-vous anglais ? – Do you speak English?

Transport and Directions

- Un aller-retour pour Chamonix, s'il vous plaît – A return ticket to Chamonix, please

- À quelle heure part le prochain bus ? – What time does the next bus leave?

- Où est la gare ? – Where is the train station?

- Où est le téléphérique ? – Where is the cable car?

- Faut-il des pneus neige ? – Are snow tires required?

Skiing and Outdoor Activities

- Je suis débutant(e) – I am a beginner

- Je suis confirmé(e) – I am advanced

- Plus lentement, s'il vous plaît – Slower, please

- Plus vite – Faster

- Où est la location de skis ? – Where is the ski rental?

Hiking and Mountain Safety

- Le sentier est-il balisé ? – Is the trail marked?

- Combien de temps pour aller au refuge ? – How long to the mountain hut?

- Je suis perdu(e) – I am lost

- Pouvez-vous m'aider ? – Can you help me?

- Y a-t-il de l'eau potable ? – Is there drinking water?

- Où est le refuge le plus proche ? – Where is the nearest hut?

Emergencies and Health

- J'ai besoin d'un médecin – I need a doctor

- Appelez une ambulance ! – Call an ambulance!

- Accident, nous avons besoin d'aide – Accident, we need help

- Avalanche, secours ! – Avalanche, help!

- Où est la pharmacie la plus proche ? – Where is the nearest pharmacy?

Everyday Practicalities

- Où sont les toilettes ? – Where are the toilets?

- Puis-je payer par carte ? – Can I pay by card?

- Pouvez-vous l'emballer sous vide pour le voyage ? – Can you vacuum-pack it for travel?

- Quel est le mot de passe du Wi-Fi ? – What is the Wi-Fi password?

The Human Side of Effort

Some travelers worry their French is too limited to matter, but in truth, it is not about fluency. It is about the effort. Locals in ski resorts are used to English speakers, yet they recognize when a traveler makes the smallest attempt in French. Often, after you try, they will switch to English to make things easier. But because you tried first, the exchange feels warmer, more genuine.

These moments linger in memory. The cheesemonger who smiles as you say *"Puis-je goûter?"* The waiter in Annecy who encourages your hesitant French as you order dessert. The hikers who greet you on a quiet trail. These are not just transactions but small bridges of connection. The Alps may dazzle with landscapes, but it is these human encounters, shaped by language and etiquette, that leave the deepest mark.

Bonus 2: Itineraries for Every Traveler (3–7 Days)

Traveling through the French Alps is never a one-size-fits-all experience. Each visitor comes with a unique lens: some seek snowy slopes and adrenaline, others crave quiet villages, while many want to balance lakeside strolls with fine dining. To help you shape your own journey, this chapter presents flexible itineraries for different types of travelers, ranging from quick three-day getaways to immersive weeklong adventures. Whether you are traveling solo, with family, as a couple, or with friends, the following plans are designed to inspire, adapt, and make the most of your time in this stunning alpine world.

A Three-Day Alpine Getaway

A short visit calls for focus. Three days is just enough to capture the atmosphere of the Alps without rushing too much. This itinerary works best for those flying into Geneva or Lyon, as both cities connect easily to major alpine towns.

Day 1: Arrival and Alpine First Impressions
Arrive in Annecy, the jewel known as the "Venice of the Alps." Spend your morning walking along its canals, exploring the old town with pastel-colored façades, and tasting a slice of *tartiflette* for lunch. In the afternoon, take a boat ride on Lake Annecy for panoramic views of mountains mirrored in the water. Dinner at a lakeside restaurant sets the tone for your trip. Overnight in Annecy.

Day 2: Chamonix and Mont Blanc Adventures
Take an early train or drive to Chamonix. Start with the Aiguille du Midi cable car, which whisks you up to dizzying heights with direct views of Mont Blanc. Adventurous travelers can walk the glass skywalk "Step into the Void." In the afternoon, stroll through Chamonix village, shop for alpine gear, and relax in a café. In winter, try a few ski runs; in summer, take a short hike in the surrounding

valleys. Return to Annecy or spend the night in
Chamonix for variety.

Day 3: Cultural and Relaxing Finale
 On your last day, head to Aix-les-Bains, a spa town
on Lake Bourget. Enjoy a morning of thermal baths,
followed by a leisurely lakeside walk. If time allows,
visit the Château de Bourdeau overlooking the
water. Return to your departure city in the evening.

This itinerary blends city charm, alpine adventure,
and relaxation—ideal for travelers short on time but
eager for variety.

Four-Day Outdoor Adventure Escape

Four days allow for more activity and immersion in alpine landscapes, making this itinerary ideal for active travelers.

Day 1: Geneva to Chamonix
Land in Geneva and transfer directly to Chamonix. Spend your afternoon exploring the town, adjusting to the altitude, and enjoying hearty alpine cuisine. Try fondue in a rustic chalet for dinner.

Day 2: Mont Blanc Exploration
Take the Aiguille du Midi cable car for sweeping views, then continue with the Panoramic Mont-Blanc gondola that crosses into Italy (seasonal). Hike a moderate trail such as the Grand Balcon Nord. Return to Chamonix in the evening.

Day 3: Lake Annecy Adventures

Travel to Annecy for a day of water and leisure. Rent a bike to circle the lake, stop at local beaches, and swim if the season allows. Alternatively, take a paddleboard or kayak out on the water. End the day with dinner in Annecy's old town.

Day 4: Departure via Grenoble or Lyon

Spend your final morning in Grenoble, known as the "Capital of the Alps." Ride the cable car to La Bastille for panoramic views of the city framed by mountains. Catch a train or flight out in the afternoon.

This plan is best for adventure lovers who want equal doses of hiking, water sports, and alpine panoramas.

Five-Day Romantic Escape

Perfect for couples, this itinerary mixes charming villages, lakeside walks, and cozy evenings.

Day 1: Arrival in Annecy
Begin in Annecy, where romantic canals and flower-lined streets set the mood. Enjoy dinner at a candlelit restaurant by the lake.

Day 2: Lake Annecy Day
Spend the day cruising on the lake or renting a private boat. Stop in Talloires, a picturesque village known for its gourmet restaurants and secluded shores. Share a wine tasting in the evening.

Day 3: Chamonix Adventure for Two
Take a day trip to Chamonix. Ride the Montenvers train to see the Mer de Glace glacier. Have lunch with a mountain view, then stroll hand-in-hand through boutiques before returning to Annecy.

Day 4: Aix-les-Bains Thermal Retreat

Travel to Aix-les-Bains and spend the day indulging in spa treatments. Many resorts offer couples' packages. In the evening, walk along Lake Bourget's promenade.

Day 5: Farewell in Chambéry

End with a stop in Chambéry, a small but beautiful city rich in Savoyard history. Explore the medieval old town, then enjoy a final Savoy wine tasting before departure.

This five-day journey is all about slowing down and savoring, balancing mountain grandeur with quiet lakeside charm.

Six-Day Family-Friendly Discovery

Traveling with children requires a mix of activities that keep both parents and kids engaged. This plan balances outdoor fun, educational stops, and downtime.

Day 1: Arrival in Geneva and Transfer to Annecy
Check into a family-friendly hotel. Spend the evening walking the old town and enjoying crêpes for dinner.

Day 2: Lake Annecy Activities
Rent bikes with child trailers and cycle part of the lake's scenic route. Spend the afternoon at a family-friendly beach such as Plage d'Albigny, where kids can swim and play.

Day 3: Day Trip to Chamonix
Children will love the Montenvers cog railway to the Mer de Glace. Visit the glacier ice cave and learn about climate change in the Glaciorium. Return to Annecy for the night.

Day 4: Grenoble Science and Culture

Head to Grenoble and visit the Musée de Grenoble or the Bastille Fortress, accessible by cable car. The ride itself is a highlight for children. Have a relaxed dinner in town.

Day 5: Chartreuse Regional Park

Explore easy hiking trails in the Chartreuse mountains, ideal for children. Enjoy a picnic surrounded by meadows and cows. In the evening, stay in a countryside guesthouse.

Day 6: Aix-les-Bains and Departure

Spend your last morning by Lake Bourget, with options for a short boat ride. Parents can enjoy a quick thermal spa session while kids play at lakeside parks. Depart from Geneva or Lyon.

This itinerary creates memories for all ages while keeping logistics simple.

A Seven-Day Alpine Highlights Tour

A week allows you to experience the Alps in full: lakes, mountains, culture, and cuisine.

Day 1: Geneva to Annecy
Arrive and settle in Annecy. Evening stroll and dinner by the canals.

Day 2: Exploring Annecy
Morning boat ride, afternoon cycling around the lake. Dinner in Talloires.

Day 3: Chamonix and Mont Blanc
Day trip to Chamonix with Aiguille du Midi and glacier exploration. Overnight in Chamonix.

Day 4: Hiking in Mont Blanc Region
Choose a half-day trek such as the Lac Blanc hike. Evening return to Chamonix village.

Day 5: Grenoble City Break
Transfer to Grenoble. Explore La Bastille and enjoy the city's lively food markets. Overnight in Grenoble.

Day 6: Aix-les-Bains
Relax at thermal spas and explore Lake Bourget. In the evening, enjoy local wines and cheeses.

Day 7: Chambéry and Farewell
 Final stop in Chambéry. Wander its old town, then return to Geneva or Lyon for departure.

This one-week tour strikes a balance between iconic attractions and slower moments, ensuring you see the best of the Alps without exhausting yourself.

These itineraries are guides, not strict rules. The Alps are diverse, and weather often plays a role in planning. Winter visitors might swap hiking for skiing or snowboarding, while summer travelers might replace spa days with lake swims. Transportation also shapes each journey: trains and buses connect most major towns, but having a car allows greater flexibility for villages and mountain trails.

Budget also influences choices. A traveler staying in luxury chalets will have a different rhythm than a backpacker camping in the summer. Fortunately, the French Alps offer both ends of the spectrum and everything in between. The key is balance: mix adventure with rest, and cultural discovery with personal indulgence.

Bonus 3: Digital Nomads in the Alps: Work & Explore

The French Alps are no longer just a playground for winter skiers and summer hikers. In recent years, they have become an unexpected haven for digital nomads who want to balance work with adventure. Picture yourself finishing a video call with colleagues, then stepping outside to crisp mountain air and views of snow-dusted peaks. For remote workers, the Alps provide a unique blend of high-quality lifestyle, stunning natural surroundings, and access to both quiet retreats and vibrant towns. This chapter explores everything a digital nomad needs to thrive here, from reliable workspaces and connectivity to lifestyle choices and practical tips.

Why the Alps Work for Digital Nomads

Working remotely often means choosing places that combine stability with inspiration. The French Alps stand out because they provide both. High-speed internet is increasingly available, even in smaller mountain towns, thanks to fiber-optic rollout and strong 4G and 5G coverage. Many Alpine towns cater to international visitors year-round, offering coworking spaces, cafés, and accommodations designed for longer stays. At the same time, nomads can easily step into nature, from skiing in Chamonix to cycling around Annecy or hiking in the Vanoise National Park. The Alps also have good transport links to cities like Geneva, Lyon, and Grenoble, making it easy to stay connected to major travel hubs.

Internet, Connectivity & Workspaces

For remote work, connectivity is non-negotiable. Most Alpine towns now have strong coverage, but speeds vary depending on location and season. Here's what to expect:

- **Coworking Spaces**: Towns like Annecy, Grenoble, and Chamonix have established coworking hubs. These spaces offer fast Wi-Fi, shared desks, private meeting rooms, and a community of freelancers and entrepreneurs. Prices typically range from **€15–25 per day** or **€150–250 per month**.

- **Cafés with Wi-Fi**: In larger towns, many cafés double as informal workspaces. Ordering a coffee or light meal allows nomads to work for a few hours, though peak tourist hours can get noisy.

- **Long-Stay Accommodation with Workspace**: Some chalets, hostels, and boutique hotels now market themselves as "work-friendly," advertising desk setups, reliable Wi-Fi, and quiet zones. Airbnb listings often highlight fiber internet availability.

- **Mobile Data**: A French SIM card with data packages can be a lifesaver in remote areas. Expect to pay around **€20–30 per month** for generous 4G/5G plans.

Best Bases for Digital Nomads

Not every Alpine town is equally suited for nomadic life. Some strike a better balance between facilities, atmosphere, and affordability.

- **Annecy**: Known as the "Venice of the Alps," Annecy combines lakeside beauty with a dynamic city atmosphere. Coworking hubs, good transport links, and plenty of cultural activities make it ideal for nomads seeking urban comforts.

- **Chamonix**: A favorite for adventure lovers. While more expensive than smaller towns, Chamonix offers an international community, coworking spots, and endless outdoor activities.

- **Grenoble**: A larger city nestled among peaks, Grenoble is both a student hub and a tech center. It has multiple coworking offices, vibrant cafés, and a strong expat community.

- **Smaller Villages (e.g., Samoëns, Morzine, or Briançon)**: For those seeking slower living, smaller mountain villages provide tranquility and immersion in local culture. Options for workspaces are fewer, but accommodations often include home offices and strong internet.

Balancing Work and Adventure

One of the biggest appeals of the Alps for digital nomads is the ease of mixing work with exploration. A structured approach helps maintain productivity:

- **Morning Work Sessions**: Many nomads choose to start their workday early, tackling deep-focus tasks while the mountain air is crisp.

- **Afternoon Adventures**: Once core work is done, afternoons can be dedicated to skiing, paragliding, hiking, or cycling.

- **Evening Networking**: After active afternoons, evenings are perfect for socializing in local bars, trying traditional Alpine dishes like fondue, or joining events at coworking spaces.

Practical tip: Time-zone alignment matters. France is on Central European Time (CET), which works well for collaborations with Europe and Africa. For nomads working with North America, evenings often become prime meeting hours.

Lifestyle, Budget & Cost of Living

Life in the Alps can be tailored to different budgets.

- **Accommodation**: Private rentals and Airbnb in major towns cost **€700–1,200 per month** for small apartments. Shared housing or long-stay hostels may cost **€400–600 per month**. Luxury chalets with home-office amenities range from **€2,000–3,000+ per month**.

- **Food & Dining**: Self-catering is affordable, with groceries costing around **€50–70 per week** for one person. Eating out in a mid-range restaurant is about **€15–25 per meal**, while casual bakeries and cafés offer budget options.

- **Transport**: Local buses and trains are affordable, with regional passes around **€60–100 per month**. Owning or renting a car can be useful in more rural areas but adds costs.

- **Leisure**: Ski passes vary widely. A day pass costs **€40–70**, while seasonal passes can exceed **€800–1,200**. Hiking, swimming in lakes, and exploring markets are budget-friendly alternatives.

Community & Networking

The digital nomad scene in the Alps is growing, though it remains smaller than in coastal hubs. Still, community networks exist:

- **Meetup Groups**: Many towns host regular meetups for remote workers, whether through coworking hubs or local expat associations.

- **Language Exchange Events**: Great for practicing French while meeting locals.

- **Outdoor Clubs**: Hiking, cycling, or climbing groups often welcome newcomers, creating a blend of social and active experiences.

- **Seasonal Festivals**: From Annecy's Venetian Carnival to mountain food festivals, these events create opportunities to connect beyond work.

Practical Tips for Nomads

- **Plan for Seasonality**: Winters can bring higher prices and crowded resorts. Spring and autumn are quieter, more affordable, and ideal for work-life balance.

- **Pack Smart**: Bring layered clothing suitable for both desk work and sudden outdoor adventures. Good walking shoes are a must.

- **Insurance**: Ensure your travel or health insurance covers mountain activities, not just basic care.

- **Learn Basic French**: While English is widely spoken in tourist hubs, a little French goes a long way in smaller towns.

The Alps may not be the first destination people think of for digital nomadism, but they offer something unique: a lifestyle where productivity meets adventure. The combination of fresh air, inspiring landscapes, and a growing remote-work infrastructure makes it possible to balance deadlines with downhill runs or lakeside strolls.

Bonus 4: Future of Alpine Tourism: What's Coming in 2025–2026

The French Alps have always been at the forefront of European tourism, blending natural beauty, cultural richness, and world-class outdoor recreation. Yet, the way travelers experience these mountains is constantly evolving. Global trends such as climate adaptation, sustainable tourism, digital innovation, and shifting traveler expectations are reshaping the Alpine landscape. In 2025 and 2026, visitors will encounter not only the timeless charm of snowy peaks and quaint chalets but also new approaches to hospitality, mobility, and conservation. This chapter explores the future of Alpine tourism and highlights what travelers should expect in the coming years.

Climate Adaptation and the Changing Seasons

The French Alps are deeply affected by climate change, and local authorities, businesses, and communities are taking steps to adapt. Rising temperatures mean shorter snow seasons, shifting patterns of snowfall, and an increased focus on year-round tourism. By 2025–2026, travelers can expect:

- **Diversified Resorts**: Many ski areas are broadening their offerings to include mountain biking, hiking, yoga retreats, and cultural festivals to ensure year-round activity. Resorts like Les Deux Alpes and Tignes are investing in glacier preservation but also building attractions beyond skiing.

- **Artificial Snow and Snow Farming**: While controversial, snow-making technology is becoming more sophisticated. Some resorts are experimenting with "snow farming," where snow is collected and preserved under insulating blankets for use the following winter.

- **Rise of Green Seasons**: Expect a stronger emphasis on spring, summer, and autumn tourism. Activities like wildflower hiking, e-bike tours, trail running, and alpine lake swimming are promoted to balance out winter dependency.

For travelers, this means more opportunities to experience the Alps outside of traditional ski holidays, with new itineraries centered on wellness, gastronomy, and culture.

Innovations in Alpine Accommodation

Accommodation in the French Alps is undergoing a transformation, blending sustainability with high comfort. By 2025–2026, travelers will find:

- **Eco-Lodges and Carbon-Neutral Chalets**: New lodges are being built with local timber, solar panels, and geothermal heating. Many resorts aim for carbon neutrality by 2030, but early adopters are already setting the standard.

- **Smart Chalets**: Integration of digital tools like energy-monitoring systems, smart lighting, and app-based concierge services is becoming common, allowing guests to customize their stay while reducing environmental impact.

- **Alternative Stays**: Glamping in yurts, treehouses, or glass domes overlooking the peaks is growing in popularity. These unique accommodations cater to travelers seeking immersive, close-to-nature experiences.

- **Extended Stay Options**: With the rise of remote work, accommodations are offering long-stay packages complete with high-speed internet and co-living communities for digital nomads and seasonal workers.

This shift ensures that whether you are a solo adventurer, a couple seeking romance, or a family needing comfort, there will be a future-ready option tailored to your lifestyle.

Smarter Mobility and Transport Developments

Access and mobility are central to tourism, and by 2025–2026, traveling through the Alps will become more seamless and eco-conscious. Expect:

- **Electric Transport Networks**: Many Alpine towns are expanding electric shuttle services and car-sharing platforms. Expect more charging stations for electric cars, especially around Chamonix, Annecy, and Grenoble.

- **Rail Expansion**: High-speed train services are being improved to reduce reliance on short-haul flights. The Lyon–Turin rail project, though still under development, symbolizes the region's long-term commitment to sustainable travel.

- **Cable Cars and Gondolas**: Resorts are expanding interconnected gondola networks, reducing car congestion and making it easier to hop between villages. For example, connections between Morzine and Avoriaz are being upgraded.

- **Cycling Infrastructure**: E-bike tourism is on the rise, and new cycle lanes, rental hubs, and charging stations are being built to encourage eco-friendly exploration.

Travelers will be able to move between destinations with greater ease, whether they prefer to arrive by train, cycle along alpine routes, or use clean-energy shuttles.

Tech and Digital Innovation in Tourism

The digital era is shaping how travelers explore the Alps. By 2025–2026, several innovations will define the experience:

- **Augmented Reality Guides**: Apps are being developed to overlay cultural, historical, and ecological information on landscapes when viewed through a smartphone. Imagine pointing your phone at Mont Blanc and instantly accessing facts about climbing history or local geology.

- **Virtual Trail Previews**: Resorts are introducing virtual previews of ski slopes and hiking routes, helping visitors choose trails that match their skill level.

- **Smart Tickets and Passes**: Digital ski passes linked to smartphones or smartwatches are replacing paper tickets. They can also combine with local transport and activity passes for seamless planning.

- **AI-Personalized Itineraries**: Some platforms are now offering trip planning tools that adapt recommendations in real time based on weather conditions, crowds, and personal preferences.

- **Remote Work Facilities**: Enhanced Wi-Fi coverage and coworking spaces even in smaller resorts mean nomads can work in the morning and hit the slopes in the afternoon.

This digital layer does not replace the raw beauty of the Alps, but it helps travelers make smarter choices and enjoy safer, more personalized trips.

Culinary and Cultural Tourism Trends

Food and culture are becoming just as important as outdoor sports in drawing visitors to the Alps. In 2025–2026, expect:

- **Farm-to-Table Dining**: More restaurants are sourcing directly from local farmers and cheesemakers, highlighting Alpine specialties like Tomme de Savoie, Beaufort cheese, and regional wines.

- **Food Trails**: Culinary itineraries are being created, where travelers can follow mapped routes connecting dairies, vineyards, and mountain farms.

- **Alpine Wellness and Spa Tourism**: Hot springs, thermal spas, and wellness retreats are blending traditional Alpine therapies with modern health trends, catering to both luxury travelers and those seeking relaxation.

- **Cultural Revival**: Villages are investing in festivals, artisan workshops, and heritage tours to showcase Alpine identity beyond skiing. Events such as the Fête des Guides in Chamonix or traditional cheese fairs in Savoie are expanding in scope.

This diversification makes the Alps more inclusive for travelers who want to savor local traditions as much as they want to ski or hike.

Sustainable Tourism and Green Commitments

The future of Alpine tourism will be defined by sustainability. By 2025–2026, green initiatives will be increasingly visible:

- **Zero-Waste Resorts**: Some resorts are introducing strict recycling programs, banning single-use plastics, and offering refill stations for water bottles.

- **Carbon Offsetting**: Many accommodations and ski operators now include carbon-offset programs in their pricing. Guests may also be invited to contribute to local reforestation projects.

- **Wildlife Protection**: Conservation areas are expanding, and guided tours often include an educational component about fragile ecosystems. Expect opportunities to support rewilding projects or volunteer with local NGOs.

- **Green Certifications**: Eco-labels like the European EcoLabel and Green Globe are becoming common indicators for environmentally conscious accommodations and operators.

Travelers in 2025–2026 will be part of a larger effort to ensure the Alps remain a thriving ecosystem for future generations.

Travelers of the Future: What to Expect

With all these changes, what will the traveler of 2025–2026 encounter in the Alps?

- **Families** will find more child-friendly, non-ski options such as interactive museums, safe cycling paths, and nature workshops.

- **Adventurers** will still have world-class skiing and mountaineering, but with additional activities like via ferrata, canyoning, and paragliding tailored to different skill levels.

- **Luxury Travelers** will enjoy carbon-neutral chalets, gourmet dining experiences, and spa retreats designed around well-being.

- **Budget Travelers** will benefit from hostels and affordable eco-lodges, alongside free or low-cost activities like hiking and village markets.

- **Digital Nomads** will increasingly find work-friendly accommodations with fiber internet and coworking networks.

The Alps are evolving into a destination that serves a broader range of travelers without losing the authenticity of mountain life.

Looking Beyond 2026

While this guide focuses on 2025–2026, the innovations underway point to an even longer-term transformation. Climate resilience, cultural preservation, and digital integration are at the core of Alpine strategy. Travelers can expect the French Alps to remain not only a place of recreation but also a model for how fragile ecosystems can adapt to modern tourism demands.

The mountains are timeless, but the way we experience them is not. For those visiting in the coming years, the French Alps promise a travel experience that feels both familiar and refreshingly new, rooted in tradition yet forward-looking in its embrace of sustainability, technology, and inclusivity.

Bonus 5: Traveler Resources: Apps, Websites & Local Contacts

Planning a trip to the French Alps is exciting, but with so many possibilities, it can feel overwhelming without the right tools at hand. Today, technology makes it easier than ever to find your way through mountain valleys, check the latest snow report, reserve a chalet, or connect with local emergency services. Beyond apps and websites, knowing who to contact on the ground can provide peace of mind and ensure smooth travels.

This chapter gathers the essential digital and practical resources that every traveler should know before setting foot in the Alps. Whether you are a skier looking for live piste conditions, a hiker navigating alpine trails, or a family seeking safe and comfortable transport, the following recommendations will serve as your ultimate companion.

Apps for Navigation and Maps

Google Maps

Still the most reliable all-rounder for getting from point A to point B, Google Maps covers major Alpine towns, ski resorts, and mountain roads. While it works well for driving, note that coverage on smaller trails can be limited, so it's best supplemented with a hiking-specific tool.

Maps.me

An offline map app favored by hikers and backpackers. Download the French Alps region before arrival, and you'll have detailed trail networks, mountain huts, and small roads available without needing Wi-Fi.

Komoot

A favorite among cyclists and hikers, Komoot provides curated routes for mountain biking, trekking, and ski touring. Its elevation profiles help you assess how demanding your day will be.

Savoie Mont Blanc App

Created by local tourism boards, this app combines practical information, maps, and activity suggestions specific to the Savoie and Haute-Savoie regions. It is ideal for those exploring beyond the big-name resorts.

Skiing and Snowboarding Apps

FatMap

Widely used in the skiing and mountaineering community, FatMap offers detailed 3D terrain maps. Skiers and snowboarders can explore off-piste routes safely, while freeriders will appreciate avalanche zone indicators.

SkiTracks

Perfect for performance-minded skiers, this app tracks speed, distance, altitude, and even calories burned during your ski day.

Resort-Specific Apps

Many major resorts, such as Chamonix, Les Arcs, and Val d'Isère, have their own apps featuring lift opening times, piste maps, snow forecasts, webcams, and restaurant recommendations. If you know your base resort, downloading its dedicated app can be a game-changer.

Hiking and Outdoor Adventure Apps

AllTrails

Excellent for finding hiking routes suited to your ability and time frame. User reviews and photos give you a sense of trail difficulty, and GPS tracking ensures you do not stray off path.

Cairn

Designed with safety in mind, Cairn allows hikers to download maps offline and automatically notifies loved ones of your location at set intervals. Especially useful if you plan to hike solo in remote Alpine valleys.

MeteoFrance Weather App

Weather in the Alps changes quickly. The official MeteoFrance app offers region-specific forecasts, storm warnings, and avalanche risk levels. Always check it before heading outdoors.

Transport and Mobility Apps

SNCF Connect

The official app for French rail travel. It provides schedules, real-time updates, and mobile ticketing for trains connecting Alpine cities like Grenoble, Annecy, and Chambéry.

BlaBlaCar

Popular carpooling platform that connects drivers with passengers. It's affordable, eco-friendly, and a great way to meet locals while traveling between Alpine towns.

FlixBus

Budget travelers will appreciate this app for booking long-distance buses that serve many Alpine towns.

Local Bus and Ski Shuttle Apps

Many Alpine resorts, such as Tignes or Les Deux Alpes, run shuttle buses to ski lifts and nearby villages. Look for each resort's local transport app or website to plan your movements efficiently.

Accommodation and Booking Apps

Booking.com

Best for hotels, chalets, and family-friendly stays, especially if you want to filter by amenities such as spas or ski-in/ski-out locations.

Airbnb

A popular option for apartments and chalets. Many listings in the Alps are designed for groups, making it perfect for families and ski parties.

Hostelworld

For budget travelers, Hostelworld offers dormitory and affordable private options in bigger towns like Grenoble or Annecy.

Gîtes de France

A uniquely French platform specializing in rural guesthouses and mountain chalets. Ideal for an authentic Alpine experience.

Dining and Food Apps

TheFork (LaFourchette)

Allows you to book tables at restaurants across the Alps, often with discounts. Perfect for last-minute reservations after a long day on the slopes.

Michelin Guide App

If you want to explore fine dining and Michelin-starred restaurants in Alpine regions, this app provides curated recommendations.

Yelp

While not as widely used in France as in North America, Yelp can still be useful for finding quick bites or coffee stops in tourist-heavy Alpine towns.

General Travel and Utility Apps

Google Translate

Essential if you do not speak French. Offline language packs ensure you can translate menus or signs even without service.

XE Currency

Handy for international travelers, especially if you plan to hop into nearby Switzerland or Italy during your Alpine trip.

WhatsApp

The primary communication app in France. Many local guesthouses, guides, and activity providers will prefer to message through WhatsApp rather than email.

Key Websites for Planning

France Montagnes (france-montagnes.com)

The official portal for all French mountain destinations. Provides practical information, resort comparisons, and event calendars.

Chamonix.com / Valdisere.com / Les3Vallees.com

Individual resort websites are excellent for up-to-date details on lift passes, accommodations, and local services.

Auvergne-Rhône-Alpes Tourism (auvergnerhonealpes-tourisme.com)

Covers the broader region and includes cultural festivals, heritage tours, and non-skiing activities.

MeteoFrance Avalanche Bulletins

Before skiing or hiking in high mountains, always check the official avalanche bulletins on MeteoFrance's site.

Local Contacts and Emergency Numbers

When traveling in the French Alps, it's important to know who to contact in case of an emergency or if you need practical help.

- **Emergency Services (Police, Fire, Ambulance): 112** (works across the EU)

- **Mountain Rescue (PGHM – Peloton de Gendarmerie de Haute Montagne): 17 or 112**

- **European SOS Helpline: 112**

- **Medical Assistance (SAMU): 15**

- **Fire Brigade: 18**

- **Tourist Offices**: Found in every Alpine town or resort. They provide local maps, event schedules, and transport details.

- **Pharmacies**: Look for the green cross sign. Most staff speak some English and can advise on minor medical issues.

- **Consulates and Embassies**: If you are a foreign traveler, note the location of your embassy in nearby major cities like Lyon or Geneva.

Tips for Making the Most of Digital Resources

1. **Download Before You Go**: Cell service can be unreliable in remote valleys. Save maps, translation packs, and train tickets offline.

2. **Check Updates Daily**: Weather, snow conditions, and lift schedules can change rapidly. Refresh your apps each morning.

3. **Mix Global and Local Tools**: Use international platforms like Google Maps for general planning but rely on local apps for detailed ski and hiking conditions.

4. **Stay Secure**: Use trusted Wi-Fi networks and avoid entering payment details on unfamiliar websites.

5. **Balance Screen Time**: Apps are useful, but part of the Alps' magic lies in disconnecting. Use your tools wisely, but don't let them replace spontaneous exploration.

Having the right apps, websites, and local contacts can transform your trip from stressful to seamless. They empower you to travel confidently, whether you are navigating snowy passes, booking a cozy chalet, or seeking out the best fondue in town. The French Alps reward careful planning, but they also invite adventure. By combining digital convenience with local insight, you can explore safely, efficiently, and with more time left for what matters most— enjoying the beauty of the mountains.